Bulletins from Serbia

by Aleksandar Zograf

CARTOONIST'S STOMACH: SERVING AS A NATO AIRCRAFT DETECTOR

Bulletins From Serbia

by Aleksandar Zograf

ISBN 1 899866 31 0

Published in 1999 by
Slab-O-Concrete Publications
PO box 148, Hove, BN3 3DQ, UK
mail@slab-o-concrete.demon.co.uk

Printed in Great Britain by Biddles, Guilford

INTRODUCTION

by Sasa Rakezic alias Aleksandar Zograf

My dear reader,

I never intended to write the book that you have in front of you. This is, in fact, the collection of my letters written to friends after the NATO attacks against Serbia that began on March 24th 1999. At the very beginning of the campaign, NATO bombs fell on Pancevo, the town where my wife and I live. It is a quiet, if not boring little town some 20km away from Belgrade.

After the first explosions, even though I was (like everybody else) in shock, I thought that our friends, mostly from international alternative comics circles, would flood us with email messages and phone calls. Instead of explaining to everybody over and over again about what was going on, I decided to take advantage of one facet of electronic mail, which enables you to send the same message to a multitude of addresses. I continued to send these updates more or less every day, and was surprised to hear that many of our friends were actually forwarding these messages to their friends, and soon the circle of people reading the letters was growing larger and larger. Eventually, the messages were posted on many internet sites, email lists and newsletters, as well as in printed media such as newspapers and magazines. But still, I continued to write with my fellow cartoonists in mind – they are like a global tribe, and (unlike the governments who rule the countries where they live) these loveable, nerdy little book worms don't have many problems with communicating with one another.

So this book is a collection of private observations, an intimate vision of everyday reality during wartime, and not a historical or political analysis. But still, as an introduction to the situation, I'm including a text by Terry Jones, one of the brains behind *Monty Python's Flying Circus*. In my opinion, the absurdity of the situation in my country has always been close to the surrealistic imagination of the *Monty Python* show. Perhaps this is the reason why Terry was able to understand the warped logic behind this war.

NATO BOMBING FOR BEGINNERS

a summary of the crisis in the Balkans for primary school children

Excited as we all are by the loud bangs and nice bright flashes that NATO arranged to brighten up our newscasts over the last few months, we ought to occasionally remember what it's all in aid of. It's all in aid of A GOOD CAUSE, of course, but what good cause?

The nice people at NATO tell us that it's all part of a big effort to save the lives and property of the Albanians in a place called Kosovo. Apparently the nasty Serbs have been trying to get the Albanians out of Kosovo so they can have it for themselves.

So NATO hit on the whizzo idea of bombing the crap out of Kosovo and Serbia, so that: (1) that nasty Mr Milosovic would be forced to resign, (2) the Albanians in Kosovo would be left in peace to enjoy their homes, and (3) tranquility would be restored to this troubled area. Unfortunately it doesn't seem to have turned out quite as predicted.

For example, bombing the crap out of Kosovo has meant that all the observers and UN officials who were trying to stop the Serb police doing nasty things to the Albanians had to leave. So in the interval between the observers leaving and the bombing, the Serbs had ample time to do a lot more nasty things to the Albanians than they could have before.

Of course it's very important to note that bombing the crap out of Kosovo and Serbia has not made things worse for the Albanians. It would be ridiculous to imagine that dropping bombs on peoples' homes and towns could make things worse. How could it? If that nasty Mr Milosovic hadn't been an Evil Man none of this would have happened. And anyway he has acted most unfairly in using the bombing as an excuse to do all those things to the Albanians that he wanted to do in the first place!

Milosovic simply wasn't playing cricket! And, quite honestly, when one drops bombs on people in all good faith, if the other side won't play cricket then it's no fault of our's.

So, children, we mustn't go blaming any of those nice people at NATO or the Pentagon for the fact that the stream of people coming out of Kosovo had, since the bombing started, turned into a deluge on a catastrophic level. It's all Mr Milosovic's fault and I'd like you to repeat that, please.

It also seems that bombing the crap out of Kosovo and Serbia has not had quite the effect on that Mr Milosovic himself that was expected.

Now of course it was well known that, before the bombing, Mr. Milosovic's popularity inside Serbia was on the skids. Recent protests and demonstrations against his Evil Regime had been extremely successful, and the Serbian opposition to Milosovic was gaining ground. So naturally it was anticipated that bombing the crap out of Kosovo and Serbia would help these opposition groups enormously.

For some inexplicable reason, children, I have to tell you that the opposite seems to have happened. Mr Milosovic's support within Serbia rocketed to a point where he will clearly be in power well into the next millennium. Even people who were totally opposed to him before the bombing started started to support him. This is really a totally unforeseen circumstance that nobody could have predicted.

Certainly it is absolutely impossible that anyone in NATO or in any of the intelligence organisations advising the President of the United States and the Prime Minister of Great Britain could have guessed that it might happen. To have predicted such an extraordinary reaction from the Serbian people would have meant being familiar with what happened to the opposition in Germany when the Allies started bombing the crap out of Germany, or knowing about how bombing the crap out of Vietnam solidified the Vietnamese people behind their communist regime, or how bombing the crap out of Iraq helped Sadam Hussein's domestic popularity ratings!

Why on earth should anyone in charge of the NATO operation be expected to know about these sort of things? They all happened a long, long time ago, children – in some cases over ten years ago – and far away. No! The only feasible explanation for this totally perverse and unpredictable reaction to the bombing campaign must lie in the perverse and unpredictable nature of the Serbian people themselves.

If it had been the other way round, and the Serbs had been bombing the crap out of Britain, I like to think that the Brits would have kicked Blair out of office the moment the first bombs started falling on London. That's clearly what the NATO generals were expecting the Serbs to do and they cannot be blamed if it didn't happen. Stop fidgeting at the back there!

Another gob-smackingly, down-right contrary reaction to the bombing has been that instead of encouraging the opposition to Mr. Milosovic within Serbia it has actually wiped it out. Can you believe it? The evil leader of the Serbs has actually taken advantage of our kindly-meant bombing raids over his country to suppress opposition, murder dissidents, silence radio stations, gag the press and threaten anyone who opposes his regime with treachery. Is there no end to the depravity of the man? Why! If the Serbs had bombed London, I am sure Mr Blair would have welcomed criticism in the same spirit that he has encouraged Mr Simpson [a BBC journalist] to keep telling the truth about what is going on in Belgrade. Mr Blair would never dream of silencing opposition if our country were under attack – he would encourage his opponents in the media to voice their hatred of his regime (not that it is a 'regime' of course – Mr Blair's is a 'government'.)

And, finally, children, I have to tell you that we are all totally perplexed and confounded by the fact that our well-intentioned bombing raids do not seem to have brought the peace and tranquility to this area of Europe that the NATO generals promised. They swore blind that if they were allowed to drop a few bombs in the right places, the whole thing would be over in a week and everybody would be happy.

And yet it doesn't seem to be panning out like that at all. The conflict seems to be about to spill out all over the place. Hostility and old wounds appear to have inexplicably re-opened and thousands and thousands of people are suffering for no fault of their own. The humanitarian and carefully worked out strategy of bombing the crap out of Kosovo and

Serbia even seems to have given a big boost to the nationalist far-right in Russia – so that a Third World War has even been talked about. People all over the world are terrified that global conflict is in the offing, that the world order in which the United Nations acted as a final arbiter of justice has collapsed and chaos has replaced it. Quite honestly, children, I don't want to worry you, but a lot of us are at our wits end!

So please, children, can you help us out? I'm sure you've just as much idea of how to handle this situation as the NATO generals or, come to that, the majority of our politicians.

Terry Jones, 1999

Sasa Rakezic a.k.a Aleksandar Zograf (right) and Gordana Basta (left)

ALEKSANDAR ZOGRAF: PUBLISHING HISTORY

Sasa Rakezic, drawing comics under the name of Aleksandar Zograf, first became known in the early nineties, especially to American alternative comics readers through Robert Crumb's anthology *Weirdo*. After the crisis in former Yugoslavia began, Sasa started publishing mini-format comics called *Alas!* – eight to sixteen page booklets that could be cheaply produced and posted. These strips were often reprinted in other publications anywhere in the world. The Seattle-based publisher Fantagraphics produced his first solo titles: *Life Under Sanctions* and *Psychonaut*. In Europe, Sasa's comics have been included in books and magazines such as *Signed By War*, *Sperminator* and *Stripburger*; Jochen Enterprises publishes the German *Psychonaut* series; Schizzo Presenta produced a one-off called *Diaro;* and Slab-O-Concrete published his first solo square-bound book *Dream Watcher*. Back in the USA Kitchen Sink Press put out *Flock of Dreamers*, co-edited with Bob Kathman, an anthology exploring dreams in comic form. More recently Monsterpants comics has released the third english-language issue of *Psychonaut*.

BULLETINS FROM SERBIA

Regards from the "living target" (ha ha!)
Wed, 24 Mar 1999 15:59:19

Yes, we have heard that American planes have left the military airports in Britain. They should start bombing targets in Serbia when the night falls (probably). Here, it is a sunny day, it looks like a perfectly normal working day. My parents, living near the military barracks here in Pancevo, said that tanks and military vehicles were riding all night.

You know, the whole thing is absolutely absurd, and the whole operation will be just a big slaughter. After the bombing, Milosevic will become much stronger, as he will gain all the control. They already closed the independent radio station (B92) in Belgrade, and kept their founder in prison until this morning – and this all happened before a single bomb was dropped!

You know, the things with urban, young Serbian people like me are very bad at the moment, as they have to fear NATO strikes, and they have to fear Milosevic's regime – which wants to draft them or imprison them, or waste their life in other ways. And then, if you get drafted (sometimes by force), the Albanians will shoot at you, or you will have to "fight" against the mighty NATO killing machine.

At the moment local independent radio station (Radio Pancevo) is broadcasting the program of B92, but that is just temporary, I believe. Anyway, I know a lot of people who are trying to stay away from this madness one way or another. And we are all in contact and giving some hope to each other. It will be an "art" to stay normal in this situation, but that is exactly what Gordana and I want to do.

Thanks for writing, I will inform you about how things are developing if possible.

Bye S.

Regards from your friends in Serbia!!
Wed, 24 Mar 1999 23:19:56

Dear friends, I am writing this during the raids. NATO has struck Pancevo, as well as some nearby villages, and some suburban parts in Belgrade, and many other towns in Serbia and Monte Negro. Gordana and I decided that we will stay in our flat. I tried to send a message one hour before, and was interrupted by an explosion. It was NOT in our part of town, but they hit the UTVA – a plane factory – the same one that I spoke about in *Alas* #3 several years ago. But this time, they haven't dropped bombs at UTVA factories in our neighborhood, but on their buildings in the other part of the town. I can still see the fire as I am writing this. But don't worry! We are OK by now. The guys from TV Pancevo (local TV) have been there, and they have already broadcast scenes INSIDE the building in flames! No one has been hurt at that location, as far as we know by now.

We heard emergency sirens for the last time about 20 minutes ago. Many people are still on the street, we were surprised that the panic was not overwhelming. God, it's so prosaic. I just saw some 16 or 17 year old kids on the swings in the little park nearby our block. And that flame in the distance as well. This is so stupid.

The guys from NUP (the band from the neighboring village) called 20 minutes ago, and they said HI! to all our mutual friends. It is very hard to get a line if you try to phone. In the near by village of Kacarevo there were some hits, but we still don't know what happened.

I don't know if I will be able to send MORE messages, or if I will even be able to connect, but we just wanted to say that you do not have to worry and that we are OK.

Love to you all Sasa and Gordana

NATO strikes again
Thu, 25 Mar 1999 04:27:49

Hey – The emergency in Pancevo has not stopped since the beginning of the NATO strikes at 20.00h. Gordana and I are still in our flat, we haven't been to the shelter, we were sleeping in our clothes when about ten minutes ago (at about 03.40h) we were woken up by an explosion. They just said on the radio that two places in town that were hit already had been bombed again! It's hard to understand why, the firemen had put out the fire a few hours ago, and they said that everything was already destroyed in one of the places (the UTVA airplane factory).

They showed people on the local TV again, and the roof of their house was demolished by a previous bombing – they don't even know what happened, as they were hiding in the shelter. (They were not as stupid as we are). It seems that something fell off the plane or from the bomb or missile, and made a large hole in the roof of their house. But there was nothing around, not a trace of a piece of bomb or anything.

The problem is that it is really hard to call by a phone, you can not easily get through, so I guess that there is still not all the information about what has happened. It was not even possible to call the ambulance service, so they had to announce some alternative phone numbers.

It is hard to tell what this NATO operation really means. It will DEFINITELY make Milosevic even more powerful than at the moment, because common people feel the rage because of all this, and all sort of extremism will be empowered. They will use this situation to fight the "different voices" in Serbia. They closed the most important independent radio station in Belgrade (B92) before the NATO strikes even began. And the right-wingers at the Serbian parliament asked to punish all the "defeatists and traitors" etc.

For me, it is still funny that I had a hypnagogic vision of the bombs exploding in my town long before the war in Ex-Yugoslavia even began (see *Alas! Comics* #3). And I STILL don't understand why they are

ALAS! COMICS

#3 · 2$

WEIRD HALF DREAM EXPERIENCE
by ALEKSANDAR ZOGRAF

IN 1992., THE AMERICAN ADMINISTRATION SPOKE IN FAVOUR OF BOMBING THE STRATEGIC TARGETS IN SERBIA AND MONTENEGRO, AFTER THE SERBIAN GOVERNMENT WAS ACCUSED OF HELPING THE BOSNIAN SERBS. ①

ONE OF THE TOWNS MENTIONED AS A POSSIBLE TARGET FOR BOMBING WAS PANCEVO, THE PLACE WHERE I LIVE. WE WERE LUCKY, THOUGH, THAT THE IDEA OF BOMBING SERBIA WAS REJECTED AFTER SOME TIME. YET, I'M STILL KEEPING A BIZZARE SOUVENIR: THE INSTRUCTIONS ON WHAT WE SHOULD DO IN THE CASE OF BOMBING—I FOUND IT STUCK TO THE WALL OF OUR APARTMENT BUILDING.

"DURING YOUR STAY IN THE SHELTER, YOU ARE NOT ALLOWED TO MOVE AWAY, NOR TO BRING IN DOMESTIC ANIMALS, SMOKE, USE ALCOHOL, MAKE NOISE, ETC." ②

FUNNILY ENOUGH, MY FLAT IS PRETTY CLOSE TO THE AREA WHERE BOMBS COULD FALL. FROM MY WINDOW, I CAN SEE THE PANCEVO INDUSTRIAL ZONE (WHERE SOME COMPONENTS FOR THE MILITARY WEAPONRY ARE BEING PRODUCED).

③

MAYBE NATO BOMBERS WOULD ACT VERY PRECISELY, SO THAT THE NEARBY CIVILIAN BUILDINGS AND HOUSES WOULD NOT BE HARMED. BUT HOW CAN YOU TELL?

④

STRANGEST OF ALL, I EXPERIENCED A WEIRD HALF-DREAM HALLUCINATION SOME 3 OR 4 YEARS BEFORE THE WAR EVEN STARTED, DURING THE TIMES WHEN YUGOSLAVIA WAS REALLY A SAFE AND QUIET PLACE TO LIVE.

⑤

WHILE I WAS WAKING FROM MY SLEEP, I WAS OVERWHELMED BY A SENSATION THAT A BOMB FELL JUST IN FRONT OF OUR BLOCK OF FLATS. I DIDN'T ASK MYSELF HOW IT WAS POSIBLE, I JUST WANTED SOME SHELTER ...

THEN I LOOKED OUTSIDE MY WINDOW, AND REALIZED THAT EVERYTHING WAS NORMAL. THIS INCREASED MY CONFUSION EVEN FURTHER. FOR A MOMENT, MY HALF-DREAM EXPERIENCE SEEMED EVEN MORE REAL THAN REALITY ITSELF.

THANK GOD THAT BOMBING OF MY HOMETOWN DIDN'T OCCURE IN OUR ACTUAL REALITY. STILL, I WAS WONDERING WHAT WILL BE LOST IF BOMBS DESTROYED MY FLAT? JUST A BUNCH OF SILLY CARTOONS, I GUESS...

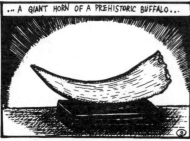

..A GIANT HORN OF A PREHISTORIC BUFFALO...

...A RUSSIAN MICKEY MOUSE MADE OF GREEN PLASTIC...

...MINIATURE SCULPTURES I CREATED SOME TIME AGO...

SOME OF THE FOSSILES I ESCAVATED, TOO!

SUCH A BEAUTY!

...AND ALL THE LITTLE USELES THINGS MY MEMORIES ARE MADE OF...

BUT THE GOOD THING ABOUT MY WINDOW VIEW IS THAT IT COULD BE SOLD TO FOREIGN REPORTERS FOR BIG MONEY!

...AND NOW, OUR BOYS ARE LEADING IN ATTACK!

$ $ $

Alas #3 • Published in 1994 as an eight page mini-booklet

bombing this stinky little town of Pancevo again and again, and how it is going to stop the conflict in Kosovo. (I just heard that Belgrade is also under heavy bombings again).

Until soon (hopefully)
Sasa and Gordana

Hello!
Thu, 25 Mar 1999 17:34:39

Hello you people! Good to hear from you again!! The snail mail system in Serbia is not functioning any more, so please do not send anything at the moment. These bombings may intensify soon, your kind words are the great encouragement for us!

I hope so much that some day we will live in a world where some other methods will be used to resolve conflict, instead of bombing.

Regards Sasa

News
Thu, 25 Mar 1999 18:51:23

Hello again! The raids stopped about 30 minutes ago, but I'm sending just brief news, etc. First of all, thanks to everybody who wrote emails!!! It means so much to us!!! Tell us what is happening out there in the "normal" world, in everyday life reality, we don't want to listen only to war reports. At this point, we decided that we will stay in our apartment on the 5th floor. IMPORTANT: please do not send snail mail as – so far as I know – it is not functioning any more in Serbia. Also, do not send "heavy" file attachments, as both electricity and phone lines are not functioning "normally", so I'm afraid that heavy files will be no good for my mailbox.

I went to see my parents (they do not have a phone at their place!) and was caught by the emergency sirens while I was riding my bike on the road near the (empty, I think) army barracks. I was surprised to see that most of the people around just continued with their everyday activities, nobody was running in panic. It turned out that Pancevo was not bombed this morning, thank God!

Nandor Ljubanovic (the guy who recently has published that *Kulturbunt* fanzine) lives only 500m and 1000m from the places where the bombs felt yesterday in Pancevo. Nandor is sending his regards to all our mutual friends, and he said he and his family are OK. During the first strike, the emergency system was not used, and he was getting out of the car, together with his sister-in-law (who is going to give a birth any day now) when they saw two flashes not so far away from them! It turned out to be NATO missiles, and they caused a spectacular explosion. During the second strike, early in the morning, Nandor went out on his terrace to light a cigarette, and the next thing that he saw was a big red flash which lit up a dark sky. The second strike was much heavier, and from my window I was able to observe a large black cloud over that place for at least 10 hours. Luckily, the fire didn't spread.

They have started to run only domestically produced, Yugoslav movies in the cinema, and boring old war movies on the TV, the same movie on all state TV channels. And still there is not enough news and not enough reliable information, but we heard that these strikes may become harder and harder…

Regards to all Sasa and Gordana

CORRECTION
Fri, 26 Mar 1999 10:41:52

Hey – I just got back from the centre of town, when the raids began again. Just a quick note to correct my note from yesterday: the postal system IS working between the raids, this far. So if anyone wants to send snail mail, it should be OK, well, at least you can try – I don't know if YOUR domestic post office has some restrictions concerning the mail to Serbia (we are "enemies", remember?). But you can try, and we will see what happens. As far as I know they already bombed some communication systems, and I don't know which "phase" of the bombing will include resources for postal services etc.

Charles Alverson, the ex-editor of legendary *Help!* magazine, and the author of scripts for some movies by Terry Gilliam, has lived in Serbia since 1994. He had a slide lecture on *Mad* and American underground comics in Pancevo seven days ago, and it was great. To all the people who know him or his work: Charles and Zivana are well, and safe – they live in a very small village in a northern part of Serbia, and there are no military bases or targets for bombings. See you later Sasa and Gordana

Mon, 29 Mar 1999 11:27:16

Dear friends, my computer has not been working, so I wasn't able to send you emails, or to write back to all of you who were so kind enough to write. I will try to convince a friend who is keen on computers to come and fix the damn thing! I heard from others that it is not easy to connect, anyway.

Yesterday we saw from the window another strike at the same spot at the UTVA airplane factory plant. How would you feel if you saw a red mushroom cloud over your home town? Still, I've got to say that it looked pretty impressive, with a lot of twinkling shiny sparks around. It caused a fire again, and about 30 houses in the surrounding area were damaged by the detonation. It's funny – our friend Nandor was in front of his apartment building, together with a couple of neighbours. They heard the aircraft, which fired a missile from someplace over their building, straight into the UTVA Factory plant. They were about 1 Km from the place of bombing. It happened at 20.50, yesterday evening.

I've been working on a comics workshop since last September, and it is called "kuhinja" (kitchen), as it happens every Saturday at the large table in our kitchen. I gathered a group of cartoonists from Pancevo, Belgrade and the towns in the surroundings. the youngest of them, Vuk Palibrk – 12 years old – called me yesterday, and asked: 'Are we going to have a workshop this Saturday?' I said 'No, it's too complicated, raids are on during the day, it's not easy to come to this part of the town, etc. Another time that kid made me laugh was when he saw Julie Doucet, who had an exhibition here in Pancevo only a month before this madness started: 'she looks better as a comic character than in real life' said Vuk. I'm sure Julie is going to kill the little bastard, as soon as she gets him!

I spoke to another cartoonist that many of you know – Wostok, he is OK, they still haven't dropped any bombs at his native town of Vrsac. On the day the strikes began, Wostok made a short video film, with his father playing STALIN!

Here we are exposed to shameless propaganda on the State TV, it is so horrible. The regime's police have closed down two independent radio stations and the police came into the Radio Pancevo offices, and forced them to 'tone down' their reports.

At the same time, it's hard to say what is happening, because we are so badly informed. They said that about 130 people died during several days of NATO strikes. Could be less, could be more, who knows? Until soon, Sasa and Gordana

```
We are back!
Tue, 30 Mar 1999 23:21:31
```

Dear friends,
Hey, the computer is fixed, so I can type messages directly to you again. Sorry, but it will take a while before I can answer all the mail. It's funny, people here seem to be more relaxed at the moment, as they are getting used to the sound of the NATO aircraft in the air, even bombing. It is scary to realize that you can get used to such things after a while. The usual target in my town (UTVA airplane factory plant, in the suburban part of Pancevo) was bombed with two projectiles yesterday evening. Mind you, the factory only produces small planes, used in agriculture, or for the extermination of mosquito larvae. As far as I know, they have never produced military airplanes, but were able to fix them (or some

parts, perhaps) at their plant, so maybe that was why NATO has been bombing that spot so often. Oh, I never was quite able to understand all those technical things.

The raids are not such big news here. The shelters and basements are mostly full of elderly people, and children. The others prefer to stay at home, if they are not too close to the "targets", etc. People with children are really worried, because some of the children are really frightened by the situation, and it is very hard to give them a sensible explanation about what is really going on. In fact, most of the grown-ups are confused as well…

I spoke to Vladimir Nedeljkovic, one of the guys from my "kitchen" comics workshop, and a leader of the band called Zontag. His wife is 6 months pregnant, carrying twins. As soon as the bombing of Pancevo began, they moved to Vrsac, as it is still a much calmer place. Vladimir told me that, during one of the NATO attacks, while his father was in a basement of his house in Pancevo, burglars came in and tried to rob the house. Vladimir's father took a gun and shot a few times in the air, and they ran away.

The program on the Serbian TV has changed during the past few days (some of the TV relays in Southern Serbia were, by the way, destroyed by bombings). I was disgusted by the propaganda and don't have the heart to watch it, but after brief inspection I noticed that now they are not only playing boring old Yugoslav war movies, but also European and American movies (including some Disney stuff!), and very popular Mexican soap operas.

One of the funniest things is that they opened the International Motor Show in Belgrade, only a day or two after NATO strikes began. One of the new models introduced there was a new and improved version of the domestically produced Yugo car, called (ironically!) "Yugo Ciao"! Workers from the city of Kragujevac, which is supposed to be one of the main targets in the 2nd wave of NATO bombings, and where this cheap and much ridiculed (especially in the US!) type of car is produced, decided to make a "living shield" –

1000's of them are gathering around the Car Factory, willing to "die with their beloved factory".

Of course, this is all too ridiculous. Serbia is a country which is already exhausted by all the turmoil which has happened over the past 8 years: civil war in Ex-Yugoslavia, economic sanctions, refugees. People are tired and confused by all these happenings, and now they are attacked by the mighty Air Forces from the rich countries, so why is anybody surprised that they became irrational and bewildered. Serbia was a sad sack of a country before the bombings, and after all, NATO strikes will be used as an excuse by the Serbian regime, because they will say: 'Look, this was a beautiful, well-run country, and then NATO came and destroyed everything'. One of the ironic things is that the hardware used by the NATO forces is worth millions of dollars. Every projectile, every bomb costs hundreds of thousands of dollars, and the bombs are dropped on about 40 targets in Serbia every day. Weren't they able to use even the smallest percentage of the money to find the non-violent solution of the conflict? It is something that requires nothing but a common sense, damn it, somebody could do it for free! Greetings Sasa

News from Pancevo
Thu, 1 Apr 1999 00:16:05

Hello again – This morning the state of emergency in our town was announced by the sound of sirens, and late in the evening while I am writing this (11PM) it is still on. I was riding my bike today all over town, and haven't noticed many people running to the shelter. Yesterday early in the morning (about 3AM) NATO airplanes bombed that very same UTVA airplane plant in Pancevo, but this time, as they reported, with a new type of projectile – one which goes UNDER the ground when it reaches the target. Does it means that they are actually shooting something that is based under the ground there? The euphoria caused by Serbian forces destroying a newly designed "invisible" NATO aircraft F-117 A is still evident. The aircraft fell in the fields near the small village in a province of Vojvodina, which is probably the most important event that has ever happened in that place. Today on national TV they showed a couple of Gypsies taking the pieces of that famous plane to a scrap metal merchant.

I'm still just drawing sketches for the future comic story which will be based on all that we are going through. I hope that later I will have the time to develop it all and do the drawings in a more relaxed atmosphere. Also, I would like to invite the cartoonists worldwide, to send me your short stories (in English, preferably) about how YOU see the hypothetical bombing of the town where you are living. Send photocopies only, on the address above. I guess that if you try to imagine this event happening to you, maybe you can understand how we feel at the moment, and you can share and learn from that experience in a way. What do you think about this idea? Also, I hope that some publishers will be interested in publishing this sort of the material?

Back to reality, I was thinking about all those different types of projectiles falling all over this country in the past week. A woman from a near by village told a friend of mine that during the first night of the bombings she went to her own backyard and saw the strangest sight: a projectile flying dozens of metres above her head, like a flashing comet, heading to Pancevo. And all that in a quiet village in the plains near the sleepy town where nothing really happened for decades. It was so fantastic.

As if they have read my yesterday's letter where I mentioned that it is hard to explain to the children what is going on, the local radio (Radio Pancevo) started to play every now and then an instruction to parents about how to relate to their children during this bombing crisis. See you in my mind's eye Sasa

NATO attacks Novi Sad
Thu, 1 Apr 1999 23:51:33

Hello people – Guess what? Yesterday they didn't drop a single bomb on Pancevo. But today early in the morning (5AM) one of the bridges in the city of Novi Sad was destroyed after a NATO attack. The bridge is very close to the centre of the town (a couple of hundred metres), and only by the strangest luck nobody was hurt. Still, the nearby museum and buildings from the historic part of the town suffered some damage. The local bus and individual cars were just about to cross when the first projectile hit the bridge just in front of them, creating a hole in the concrete. They were smart enough to turn their vehicles back before another bomb fell, and – before their eyes – the whole construction sank into the Danube.

Miroslav Mandic, the legendary performance artist and writer from Novi Sad, was in a house next to the bridge. When he heard the crashing sounds after the first bomb landed, he came close to the window to see what was happening. After the second explosion, he was lifted in the air together with the glass from the window pane. He is a very strong guy, so luckily he wasn't hurt.

The most famous of Miroslav's performance is "The Rose of Wandering" – he planned to take a trip all over European countries, without using any vehicle at all – just to walk for 10 years (from 1991 to 2001), until his route formed a drawing of a rose on the map of Europe. Unfortunately, after the war in Ex-Yugoslavia had begun, he wasn't able to continue with the project. I've met Miroslav many times, and he certainly is a man devoted to art and alternative lifestyles, and I hate to think about him being in a situation like this.

I also spoke to Kebra, singer and a leader of Obojeni Program, which is one of the most appreciated bands in Yugoslavia (Hey, Gordana and I even sang "backing vocals" on their last album. We can't sing, but we yelled when they asked us to). Kebra told me that many bombs have fallen on different targets in town, but the bridge was a sort of symbol for many people in Novi Sad. Biljana, Kebra's sister and a drummer in another band (Boye), today went to see the remains of the bridge, and couldn't hold down the tears.

The rumours are that NATO will bomb the other bridges around Novi Sad during the raids tonight. Let's hope that these are only the rumours. Regards to you all Sasa

Hello – Yesterday it was very cloudy, so it seems that they haven't dropped as many bombs as usual. Oh, well.

I was thinking about the changes that the use of internet has brought to our life. Maybe it was really visible through this war – I just read a forwarded letter about the strangest topic – it seems that somebody from Italy has somehow found out the email addresses for the pilots of the planes which are taking off from the NATO base in Aviano. The addresses were sent to friends in Serbia, and it initiated the "correspondence" (mostly consisting of offensive exchanges) between the people who are dropping bombs, and those who are living in the places where the bombs are supposed to be dropped. That's modern technology.

I saw some excerpts from the pilots' "letters", which were quite disgusting, and I can only imagine the language used by those "on the ground" who were writing to them. These things are always stupid and I like to stay away from that sort of meaningless jabbering.

Speaking of jabbering, there's a lot of it on the Serbian media, which is now almost absolutely controlled by the regime. I can't listen to one more insult based on Clinton's sex affairs, or all those patriotic songs, or any other nonsense like that. I met a guy from the local Peace Movement, and he told me – "Everything that we tried to achieve in the past several years was annihilated after the bombing began".

Today, the complete staff from the independent radio station B92 from Belgrade was kicked out from their office by the police. I can't help but feel nihilistic today. S.

Hello!!! Yesterday, several NATO projectiles were launched into buildings (administrative centres) owned by the Serbian police, in downtown Belgrade. The fire destroyed the buildings, and one of them is positioned only 100 metres from the large complex of Medical Installations, including the central town's Clinic, one of the biggest in the Balkans, where babies are born. Reporters were talking to a young mother who gave birth about one hour after the bombing. All the new born babies had to be evacuated, and the mothers, too. With that eerie fire burning in the very centre of the town. What can I say. While I'm typing this, I'm listen to the news of another bridge in Novi Sad being bombed by NATO, with civilian cars crossing the bridge at the moment of impact. Several people have been taken to the hospital, said first reports.

I had no intention of writing these letters as real "war reports", you can find that sort of thing in the regular media. I'm a cartoonist, not a war journalist or political analyst. But so many people are asking me about the Albanian refugees, and the situation in Kosovo, etc. I have never even been to Kosovo, and my town is in another part of the country, so – for a start – I don't have a first-hand account of the situation there. But YES, I know of the terrible drama of the refugees. It is a real horror and a shame, I can see no justification for the suffering of those people!!

But I will describe again what happened: after the negotiations in Paris failed, UN verifiers were withdrawn from Kosovo, and Serbia was exposed to NATO attacks. As soon as this happened, the Serbian regime, which was at the bottom of its popularity in exhausted Serbia, took total control of the state media, and the police closed down all independent media. It was presented as a necessary action because of the (truly stupid) bombing action initiated by the rich and powerful countries of the West. Bewildered and enraged by the bombing of towns and infrastructure, most of the common people in Serbia haven't protested against the actions of their own government, and the regime is seen as the only force of protection. (What sort of reaction would YOU expect in your country under the same circumstances? It is so predictable).

The situation in Kosovo was already complex and heavy – NATO's action is like putting out a fire with gasoline. First of all, the whole territory was left without independent monitoring, and of course the Serbian Police and Army forces are now fighting openly with the Albanian Militia. I heard reports of people of both nationalities being frightened and confused, and of towns where the telephone lines are out, so that people don't know what is happening. In the midst of all this, it's obvious that Serbian paramilitary groups have been added to the chaos. The next thing that I've heard is that many 1000s of Albanian people have been kicked out of their houses and sent to nearby countries. Meanwhile, there is absolutely no information about this on the Serbian media – just the reports about NATO bombings and patriotic songs. And after a few days, they started to speak about Albanian refugees, but they mostly presented it as if they were escaping NATO bombings (which were really hard on Kosovo territory).

It should be stated that all of the sides involved in this hellish conflict are lying – NATO is trying to justify its irresponsible action by using its powerful media machinery, the Serbian regime is taking advantage of its own peoples' misery to control information, and the Albanians (divided into several factions, including armed extremists) are trying to use the back-up of NATO to achieve their separatist political programs. This is just one possible vision of the situation. I'm just a stupid cartoonist, I told you.

But as far as I can see, the common people on all sides are being hurt, and they are all bleeding, they are confused and bewildered, and when everything finishes, the administration of all three "sides" in this conflict will be safe and giving speeches, while the crazy people of the Balkans will have to lick their wounds (as the Serbs say) for many years to come. It's funny, we don't even know how we came to this, I feel as if I just woke up one morning to see that bombs are falling in my neighborhood. Good night, friends, love to you all S.

Boom Boom
Mon, 5 Apr 1999 18:45:32

Hey – Last night I had that strange feeling that something was going to happen, and I couldn't sleep. When I finally fell asleep, it was early in the morning. I was woken by the ring of the phone, and it was Nandor – he was covering the 'Northern' part of the town, and I was supposed to observe what was happening in the 'South'. "They said on the radio that the refinery was bombed!" – said Nandor. Everybody was fearing that this would happen – there is a danger of ecological catastrophe in Pancevo, because of the ugly industrial zone (refinery, petrochemical and artificial fertilizers industrial plants, all next to each other) in the Southern part of town, which each of you who has visited us must remember seeing from our window. It is not only close to the centre of the Pancevo, but fairly close to Belgrade as well, and local Green Party members have been warning about the potential danger of ecological disaster for years.

Anyway, I tried to see a flame or something unusual, but there was just some white cloud hovering over the area of refinery. We understood that it was not oil that was burning – that would cause a catastrophical explosion, and this time the detonation was not strong enough even to wake us up from our sleep.

It's funny but Gordana said that shortly before the phone rang, she had a dream of a tractor on a farm. The tractor was producing something that looked like big cloud of steam. And when she woke up, she was able to observe a similar type of mist rising above the refinery. They soon announced on the radio that the cloud is not poisonous, and that it is in fact water vapour which was released after one of the plants was bombed. The steam was expanding, and it soon covered everything – when we looked through the window pane few minutes later, we just saw white fog, as if the whole world had disappeared. The local TV was showing the view from a camera placed on a tall building in the centre of town, and the screen looked completely blank. Several hours later, the fog disappeared. During the bombing, about 100 workers were inside the plant. Several people were wounded and two were killed.

In Belgrade, they bombed a large fuel tank, used for the city central heating system. Hardly a "military" facility at all, but the flame was spectacular. I guess it looked impressive on CNN?

I saw a TV report about yesterday's NATO bombing of another bridge in Novi Sad. It was a very large bridge, and there were people crossing it in cars, bicycles and by foot when the bombs fell. They are still searching for bodies in the Danube, and those who survived were describing the horrible, horrible scenes. Electric wires were falling down from the upper parts of the bridge. The aquaduct was joined to the bridge, so 1000s of people are now left without running water. What is there to say? This seems like an ordinary day to us. Now when I think of it I'm horrified. Regards from Sasa and Gordana

PS: I am trying to send this from another computer. My server is out of action at the moment, because NATO has bombed some antennae in Belgrade (I can't understand the technical details), and they hope to fix it within two days. Send any messages to my old address zograf@pancevo.com I will answer when I can.

Anniversaries
Tue, 6 Apr 1999 15:51:34

Hello, Gordana and I jumped out of bed at 3.50AM, woken by a sound of a strong explosion, coming somewhere from the North. We haven't seen a flame or explosion though. Nandor, who lives in a Northern part of the town, also wasn't able to spot the target of the bombing, even though he heard the planes and three detonations. At the time of writing this (1PM), the local radio has said that they can't locate the place where the bombs fell either!?!

This morning I was standing in the long queue in front of the local newsstand. People were waiting to buy cigarettes (five packs per customer). I don't smoke, but I wanted to buy some for Gordana and my parents. But the modest supply was sold out before my turn. There is a great shortage of cigarettes, and many people are really nervous, because, as you probably know already, people in this part of the world smoke so much. Yesterday, early in the morning, NATO bombed the city of Nis, with 15 projectiles, which caused horrible damage across the very heart of the town. The strange thing was that they bombed the plants of the tobacco industry in Nis as well. The whole storage of 100 tons of tobacco was burnt down completely.

If that is a military target, what on earth is NOT a military target?

Today it's 6th of April, the date that marks the rather ironic anniversary – on that day in 1941, Belgrade was bombed by the Nazi German Army. Everybody remembers this as an Armageddon-type event, with many 1000s of dead civilians, and institutions like the National Library completely burnt down. Bombs even fell on the Zoo which was (and still is) rather close to the centre of the city, so that wild animals were running all over the place (as shown in the movie "Underground", by Kusturica). A similar unhappy anniversary will probably be marked on April 16-17th, when, this time in 1944 – during Orthodox Easter, Belgrade (and many other towns in Serbia) – still under German occupation, were bombed by the Allies. The bombing was supposed to be targeted at German military facilities, but – due to bad weather – the bombers missed most of their targets, and mostly killed civilian people and caused great destruction in the town. It seems that these events caused people in Serbia feel as if they are being bombed by everybody, be it the Occupation Army or the Allies. Mind you, many people who went through all that hell are still alive, and they are watching the same thing happening in 1999. By the way, last night they bombed a small town of Aleksinac – one projectile hit the Army barracks, while two bombs fell on civilian houses, destroying the whole street near the centre of the town, and causing deaths and injuries of many civilian people (they're still searching for them under the ruins). It looks pretty much like WW2. This was a rather awful night in Serbia anyway, with the refinery in Novi Sad bombed and set on fire, and with the only remaining bridge in town being the target of two Tomahawk missiles. Both of the missiles were destroyed by Serbian anti-aircraft forces, but, of course, everybody will fear that the next night NATO will try to hit the same spot again.

It should not be forgotten that on 6th April in 1992 the siege of Sarajevo began, this time with Bosnian Serbs taking the role of bombers. And above all this, our friends from NATO will have to celebrate their 50th anniversary on 24th April (I think) this year. After 50 years, problems are still being "solved" by dropping bombs. As you can see, an anniversary can be a horrible thing.

Sasa

Panic in Pancevo
Wed, 7 Apr 1999 23:39:48

Hello everybody – as I told you in some previous letters, there is a great fear of ecological catastrophe in Pancevo. Every time the bombs fall most people glance in the direction of the Southern (industrial) Zone of town. And very often friends call us (because we live nearby) to ask if the Zone has been hit yet.

Today people were even more disturbed when the Mayor turned up on local radio and TV and said that we should prepare for this potential disaster, and that it is recommended that anybody who doesn't have any other obligation should leave town, or go to friends and relatives in the countryside. Even though everybody was used to all kinds of bad news during the past two weeks, this sounded like a pretty serious warning. Rumours were starting to spread all over town, and we met many people who were trying to get out of Pancevo.

They had to air a few special TV/radio announcements after that, trying to calm down the atmosphere in order to prevent panic, as it seemed that even the Mayor was not aware that people would react like that. While I write this (22.30h) the state of the emergency is on, but I can't see anybody in front of our apartment building, even though during the past few days some people from our neighborhood would usually come out of the shelters and watch the bombings or try to spot NATO aircraft (sometimes they look like a tiny, moving spot in the sky). Tonight it's unusually quiet.

Of course, people also worry because they saw that the refinery in Novi Sad (which is much smaller in size compared to this one in Pancevo) was hit TWICE, while the refinery in Pancevo has been bombed only once so far. Still, the most alarming thing would have been an incident at one of the Industrial plants next to refinery, where they deal with some poisonous gases.

Also, many of the people that I spoke to were disturbed after they heard about the bombing of 100% civilian blocks of houses in Aleksinac, a small town on the South of Serbia. Even NATO officials confirmed that it could have been a "technical mistake" or "the result of the destruction of the missile by the Serbian defence system". On TV they showed one of the people who survived the bombing. He said – "I was wondering why it ever happened. I haven't done anything. I was just sitting in my home and the next moment a bomb fell on my house". He was saying something which reflects what many of us feel.

Speaking of "mistakes" and other unusual things connected with NATO raids which were said to be strictly aimed at military targets, it was noted that several projectiles fell not only on civilian spots, but even on neighboring countries (Bulgaria, Macedonia and Albania).I am not a military expert, and I don't know what could have initiated that sort of failure, but for many it is a proof that you never know where missiles will fall, once they have been launched.

Today many people in Novi Sad went to the only bridge that remained in the city (even though that bridge was damaged by NATO projectile two days ago). People are creating a "living chain" there, in order to protect it from bombing. The same type of action has been happening on one of the bridges in Belgrade, as well.

See you soon. Sasa

It's a few minutes after 10PM already, and no emergency sirens. That's pretty odd, because we were almost getting used to NATO raids around 8 or 9PM. (Ooops, they just announced a state of emergency, at 10.15). Last night, the Oil Refinery in Pancevo was not attacked, but many people have left the town already because of the fear of ecological disaster. Gordana hoped that we would find a shop which sells cigarettes somewhere, because the queue wouldn't be so huge in the empty town. But it seems that all the supplies are sold out already. Dozens of buses prepared in case of need for evacuation are parked in parts of the town. Gordana went to her job in a near-by village, to find out that it was full of people who escaped there from Pancevo yesterday evening.

Tonight, rock bands are playing a concert on a large bridge over Danube, which connects Pancevo and Belgrade. Let's hope that it will convince NATO not to drop bombs while the people are there?

Last night the bombs fell on the Justice Court building in the very heart of Belgrade. The building was not used by the military at all, and it was a coincidence that nobody was hurt, as passers-by (despite the state of emergency) were walking there on the pavement and watched the projectiles falling from the sky on a beautiful evening.

I saw the report about bombings of a small town called Cuprija, a place that I have visited several times. I remember it as a quiet, sleepy town, and it was bizarre to see the buildings and little shops destroyed, with the articles from the boutiques spilled all over the place. As the bombing campaign progresses, more and more civilian targets have been shot, and more and more people are being killed and yet it's hard to find out about the exact number of the victims. I guess that authorities think that it will be too depressing to count deaths in a situation like this?

On the lighter side, we heard that Serbian cartoonist Ivana Filipovic has successfully moved to Vancouver, Canada. Good luck, Ivana! Also, friends from *Galago* (one of the best European alternative comics magazines) said that they are ready to come to Belgrade for the exhibition of contemporary Swedish comics scene, as soon as the war stops. The exhibition was in preparation shortly before the whole madness began. I hope to see you soon, guys. Regards Sasa

Waiting for the bombs
Sun, 11 Apr 1999 00:21:43

Hey – I'm getting weary of all this. I'm not so much of a "war" type, and can't wait for the time when I will read comics late at night, instead of standing at my window pane and watching "Tomahawk" missiles flying around. The war rhetoric on the radio and TV are enough to blow your mind. And behind our backs, so many Albanian people being kicked out from their homes in Kosovo. I've lost my will to do anything. I need some time to be left on my own.

But don't worry – soon your correspondent will collect his mind, and be ready for this bombing business, and letters and all.

Last night the radio warned of "many NATO aircraft coming from the North in the direction of Belgrade". I heard the planes, and explosions as well, but there was no news about horrible bombings as we have been used to over the past few days. For some reason, yesterday's activities of the NATO airplanes over Serbia were not so drastic.

This morning, everybody was commenting and trying to figure out – "Why haven't they dropped bombs?". While I was passing down the street, I heard some old man saying: "This must have been a provocation!".

The other night 6 projectiles hit the car factory plant in Kragujevac, while the workers were around, forming a "human shield". It was reported that 124 persons were injured. They said that they will continue with the "human shield" action. This bombing has destroyed the central heating system built not only for the internal use in the Factory, but also for the heating of the (civilian, of course) buildings and houses in the biggest town in Central Serbia.

After all, the "human shield" actions are continuing on several bridges in a few towns in Serbia. I suspect that people will become more and more suicidal as the bombing campaign progress.

Still, you may ask: why has everybody accepted Milosevic's autocratic leadership in Serbia under NATO bombs? And even though his "reign" was becoming less and less popular during past several years (hence the student and civil protests in 1996/97)? Instead of answering that, I will let you read the comparison written and forwarded to me by Terry "Monty Python" Jones.

"Dear Sir, If the old Warsaw Pact had bombed London because they didn't like Mrs Thatcher's policies in Northern Ireland, you could be certain of two things happening: 1) the whole country would have got behind Mrs Thatcher and 2) it wouldn't have helped the situation in Ireland one little bit."

That guy, Terry Jones! He's gone straight to the point. Bye Sasa

Listening
Mon, 12 Apr 1999 00:27:15

Hello. Not much bombing last night in the Northern part of Serbia, but they have bombed some targets in Kosovo and Southern Serbia, with several civilian deaths, including 11 months old baby and her father from Kursumlija, and a pregnant mother was seriously injured.

I was thinking about the fact that everybody here is trying to listen very carefully, in order to hear the planes, explosions, detonations, or whatever. Last night it was raining, and I caught myself trying to figure out if the sounds that I was hearing were thunder, NATO planes, or Serbian anti-aircraft defence.

I saw a TV report with Charles Alverson (ex-editor of Harvey Kurtzman's *Help!* magazine) joining the human shield on the only remaining bridge in the city of Novi Sad.

The other day we were at a party, and – as usual – people were talking about the situation and bombings. We heard about the old man who was so excited when he heard the emergency sirens, that he had a heart attack and died on the pavement in Balkanska street, near the centre of Belgrade.

Not so tragic was the case of the middle aged woman from Pancevo. On the first day of NATO attacks, she jumped into her car right after she heard the sirens. She drove out of town until she ran out of gas, in some distant village. She had to go back to the town by bus, during the raids, and wasn't able to return the car because they stopped selling gasoline to civilians. All sort of weird things are happening in this situation.

A friend's father had witnessed the bombings of Belgrade during World War 2, and he said that for him it was somehow easier to take: the bombings were much harder, of course, but they lasted only a day or two. After the bombing was over, if you were lucky to be alive, you had time to collect and carry on. In the present time situation, according to him, you see the infrastructure of the country being destroyed day by day, very methodically, people dying in smaller portions but in a longer period of time, horrifying TV pictures running over and over again. Still, they are announcing more and more aircraft, and the intensification of NATO strikes in the upcoming days.

Still I hope that we will live to see the better days – Regards Sasa

Refinery bombed twice
Tue, 13 Apr 1999 01:09:42

This is a second day of Orthodox Easter. What a day. First, we were woken up at about 3.30AM, by the sound of a big explosion. They bombed the oil refinery in Pancevo again! Everybody was waiting for it to happen, and so many people have already left the town, especially people with small children – because of the danger of ecological disaster. The NATO aircraft had been cruising above its target for almost 15 minutes, before the bombs were dropped – three of them. Soon the horizon was apocaliptically red. Tall flames and smoke. Burning and exploding over and over again. Still, we

The cloud in Pancevo, taken from a Serbian newspaper, the arrow marks Sasa's flat

were lucky that the wind was carrying the smoke away from the town and nearest villages, so that there was no need for evacuation. The fire was burning until the afternoon. And you could smell the smoke all the way to Belgrade until late evening. Still, this was some sort of relief, as everybody has been expecting the new bombings.

Then, shortly before 10.30PM, I heard sounds of Serbian anti-aircraft defense shooting, and heard the NATO planes. Soon, everybody went out at the terraces, cheering and yelling as it seemed that some of the NATO projectiles (or aircraft?) were destroyed. But soon when we heard another strong detonation, and realized that they had bombed the oil refinery yet again!! And once more we were lucky: even though the wind was blowing in the direction of the centre of the town, the black smoke was lifted high above the ground. While I write this, the firemen are surrounding the refinery, but they are still not active because the raids are on.

Today, one of the bridges in Grdulicka Klisura, in Southern Serbia, was hit by NATO while a train with about 50 passengers was crossing it. So far, ten people have been found dead in the coaches which were hit, and many more people have been injured.

Madness is surrounding us from all sides. Yesterday, Slavko Curuvija – the publisher of an independent daily paper and bi-weekly magazine from Belgrade, was killed in front of his apartment building in the very centre of the city. Is somebody using the state of the warfare to strangle the different voices in Serbia? Who is next?

Many questions, and I hear more detonations Bye Sasa

Oil Refinery and Monastery
Wed, 14 Apr 1999 00:24:45

Where is this leading to? The flame in the oil refinery in Pancevo was still burning after the bombing last night, when – at 5.33AM, we were woken by one of the strongest detonations yet. And soon after that, at 5.50AM, another bomb fell on the same plant, with an explosion of the same intensity. By a mere coincidence, Gordana had to go to work today a little bit later. Her bus to work passed near the oil refinery, at exactly the time of the first bombing (she works from 6AM to 2PM during the summer, but they will have to change the schedule, as it is becoming dangerous). Later, when she went to work, she found out that some of her colleagues were in the bus, when the bomb fell just 500 metres away. We will find out more "details" tomorrow.

The good thing about the last two projectiles is that, despite the very large explosions, they haven't produced a large flame or a cloud of smoke, which is dangerous for the whole town and many settlements in the surroundings. Still, everybody was shaken by so many bombings of the industrial area in Pancevo, in just two days. Some of our neighbors work at the oil refinery, and they were watching as their working spaces were being torn to pieces. During and after the war in Ex-Yugoslavia, and sanctions against Serbia, the refinery was one of the very few companies in town which was actually economically reliable.

Except for the fact that the whole complex of plants was built very close to the town, another thing which speaks about the unbelievable ignorance of the planners from Tito's era is the fact that the refinery was built around the Orthodox monastery built (according the legend) in the 13th Century!! The very sight of the old monastery surrounded by the oil refinery is one of the more surrealistic sights that you can see anywhere. Bombs exploding around it make it even more unreal. It is also rather ironic that nobody even said anything about the conditions of the monastery after the bombing, we just heard that the glass in the windows was broken, which is usual for the buildings in the immediate zone of the bombing.

Hey, I speak less and less about comics in these letters. And I don't like it.

Bye Sasa

Beautiful day?
Thu, 15 Apr 1999 01:15:46

Hello everybody – Today I went around town on my bike, and it was really a beautiful spring day. I saw a three-colored cat chasing a mouse in the grass near the refugee camp in my town. The camp (based in a complex of ex-army barracks) was full of Serbian refugees from Bosnia and Croatia, who were kicked out of their homes, only to come to a country where they have to fear bombs again. I was thinking about "parallel" realities, as I couldn't help enjoying the springtime, even though I guessed that there must be some apocalyptic type of event going on at the same time someplace else in this country. Later I saw a TV recording of a NATO bombing of the town of Valjevo – the camera stood still for maybe 15 minutes, and you could see the explosions and mushroom clouds bursting in the distance from time to time. And all the while you were able to hear birds from the near-by meadow, singing their sweet song with no interruption.

Later I saw the pictures of the convoy of poor Albanian refugees, kicked out of their homes, which were for some reason today bombed by

NATO projectiles. More than 60 people were killed. A horror. In this part of the world, everybody has to bear this absurd, stressful line of events.

Yesterday they bombed the emptied army barracks in the suburb of Belgrade. Very close to the targeted place is a hospital with many of the people (from all over Serbia) who are already injured from previous NATO bombings! The building was damaged by the detonation, and the broken glass from the windows fell on the patients, and in one of the rooms a ceiling fell on one of the hospitalized people.

As for much lighter topics, I received a mock-up version of my new comic book *Psychonaut* #3, which will come out with a small publisher in the US (MonsterPants Comics) and will be supported by a movie/video production house (Freight Films). This package with a mock-up version of the comic book was probably one of the last things that I'll receive from abroad after the beginning of this war, as the reliability of snail mail is very questionable. It's funny that I have never even been to US, even though I have many American friends, and despite the fact that most of my comics were originally published there. I thought that it is good that, while our governments are busy planning their dirty little war games, we − alternative comics people − are still collaborating and understanding each other so well. Greetings to all, Sasa

Leaflets, bombs and patriotic songs
Fri, 16 Apr 1999 01:25:23

Hello

Well, Gordana came back from work today (she works at a fruit plantation as an agriculture engineer), where they spotted leaflets falling from the sky. It turned out to be NATO propaganda leaflets, written in Serbian, with all those NATO trade marks, and the announcement: "We want to talk to you"! Ha ha, it was almost like WW2 iconography, something that we all remember from the ancient black and white movies. You would hardly expect stuff like that from the NATO sophisticates. I will keep the leaflets for my collection anyway!

On the other side, TV programs here are filled with insults and war propaganda, not too far away from the WW2 either. I still remember that, when the bombing campaign began, I heard a Serbian TV News Broadcaster calling Clinton "a semi-talented saxophone player". I was wondering – if they really wanted to be offensive, why didn't they just call him a "BAD saxophone player"?

It is all so silly. And the silliest of all are the "patriotic" songs, done in the style of "band aid", with all of the dullest pop singers posing in front of camera etc. I always found those "band aid" projects boring to tears, and on top of all the tragedy we have to watch their video clips over and over again. Not to mention the fact that even Michael Jackson, as I was informed by a friend, has already recorded a song about the Kosovo refugees. It's true what they say: war is hell!

OOPS! While I was writing this, I was interrupted by a detonation. Several NATO projectiles hit the (industrial) Southern Zone of Pancevo! This is close to our home – less than 1km away, and we felt a strong vibration, but luckily the window was still in one piece. It was dangerous because they hit the Artificial Fertilizer Factory (where they work with poisonous gases) and Petrochemical plants – during the same strike! It looked rather eerie, with three flames burning with great intensity, and just a few minutes after the sound of explosion, we saw people running to their cars, trying to get out of the place. The smoke was headed in the direction of the part of town called Topola, and the radio announcement was giving the instruction for people there to evacuate. Gordana and I went to the top of our apartment building, where the younger people gathered to watch the sad "spectacle".

Soon the economy of the town will be almost completely ruined, of course. On the radio there were news about more bridges and more industrial plants being destroyed all over the country, more people killed. Another night in Serbia.

Bye Sasa

Hello! Well, yesterday was a pretty harsh day, so I will keep this message short. After I sent you the last letter (remember: they bombed all the plants in the industrial zone of the town of Pancevo, during a single strike!), there was another attack on the refinery late at night. The poisonous gas (I forget it's name, will try to check it out tomorrow) still remained in the tanks of the petrochemical industry, but if they drop another bomb tonight it could be pretty bad, you see.

Nobody believed that NATO would REALLY bomb all those plants, as they don't have anything to do with the military – fuel for the trucks and military vehicles – or anything like that. That was the reason why the whole industrial complex kept up working more or less at full steam. The workers were evacuated into shelters, though, after the air raid sirens came on – and (thank god!) just a few people were injured after the bombs hit their targets. I didn't even wake up Gordana during the last strike and bombing of the refinery. She was so tired that she didn't even wake up after the detonation. It seemed so stupid, so unreal – to watch from the top of our apartment building all those factories burning. I felt so empty inside. The next morning, I felt as if I was beaten up or slapped in the face. I took my bike and went to the area which was bombed, trying to imagine the drama during the moments of the explosions.

I remembered that only 10 days before the strikes began , the members of my "kitchen" comics workshop gathered together to go on an "excursion" to the monastery in the oil refinery. The monastery was restored and opened for visitors only recently, and for most of us (including me) it was the first time we'd seen it from the inside. The sight of a mediaevel building captured by the polluting modern technology, and of parts of the monastery, designed for meditation and self-reflection, turned into busy refinery offices, all seemed so drastic. We made a couple of collaborative drawings, pretty apocalyptic in style and mood. Little did we know that only 10 days later this area would become the place where "doomsday" style of events would take place, and that

the poor old monastery would be damaged by bombs?! After the first bombing of the refinery, some workers were injured, some were burned, some of them had their limbs and heads torn apart. How much more apocalyptic can you get?

Anyway, everybody was disturbed by the fact that it is obvious that NATO targets are becoming less and less predictable, and that the whole bombing campaign is going out of control. There were reports of bombs falling everywhere – civilian houses, post offices, backyards, open fields, even hen-houses. OK – that is enough for now. Bye Sasa

Attractive to NATO
Sun, 18 Apr 1999 00:37:20

Hello everybody! Yesterday it was unusually quiet, even eerie in Pancevo – the town was almost emptied during the night. All of us who remained were looking at the industrial part of town, fearing that the bombing of Petrochemical plant would produce a catastrophe.

A few minutes before I started to write this message, there was a "battle" in the sky, with anti-aircraft defence forces shooting, and the roar of the airplanes. They are reporting on the radio that "activity of NATO aircraft is very busy in the sky over Belgrade", probably heading to the South of the country. The sound of the aircraft is something that you feel deep inside your stomach, and once you hear it, it's very hard to forget – it is not just a sound, it is something that you remember with your "guts".

On TV they showed a guy who was (just like many workers from Yugoslav construction companies) working in Iraq , during the NATO strikes in the Gulf War. He later went back to his native Bosnia, to a small town near Sarajevo, which was demarcated as a Serbian territory, and bombed by NATO in 1995. After that, the poor guy moved to a suburban part of Belgrade (Sremcica) which was exposed to heavy bombing a few days ago, and his house was damaged. He is a funny looking guy, and it seemed that he attracts mighty NATO forces wherever he goes.

OK, as for my own activities, more than three weeks after the strikes began, I started to work on a new comic. I can hear many detonations in the direction of Belgrade. See you later, folks! Bye Sasa

EXTRA
Sun, 18 Apr 1999 12:28:40

Shortly after I posted you my message last night, I was reading the 'response' to my letters (exposed via internet) by some anonymous 'fan': "Yoshi – You deserve what you get. Our President Clinton is a good man. If he is bombing you then you must deserve it. You Serb". I was wandering what "Yoshi" could mean, when a big blast interrupted my thoughts. It was about 1AM, and the detonation was by far the most horrible that I have experienced (yet?). All three industrial plants in the town were hit by several projectiles. The explosion turned night into day, a strange, spooky, red-light day. While it was happening I had to shut down the computer, which takes some time, damn it.

(Later I heard from a friend who said that some people were having a kid's birthday party at the basement in the centre of town, the music was loud, and all the kid's parents and friends were drunk already, but when they saw that the blast that lit up the basement window and the whole street even far away from the Industrial Zone, they were quite shaken.)

I phoned our friend Nandor (the editor of *Kulturbunt* fanzine, remember), and he was ready to get in the car and leave town, with his mother, wife and two kids. Nandor's sister-in-law gave birth to a baby boy three days ago, here in Pancevo.

Soon we were able to see people in cars, or riding bikes and motorcycles leaving the neighboring industrial area.

The biggest problem of all is, of course, the petrochemical industry – they are producing plastic material, used in the production of plastic bags, hoses etc. (nothing to do with the military equipment or anything. Except for the fact that ANYTHING could be used in the military, one way or another. They will probably use this logic as an excuse to bomb EVERYTHING, and still call it "selective"). Anyway, the regular produce of petrochemical industry requires use of the toxic material such as a gas called vinyl-chloride-monomer (I'm not sure if this is correct in English). It does not have a colour or smell, and when freed – in smaller quantities it makes you laugh hysterically, and in bigger quantities – it is a deadly poison.

After the first bombing, they were trying to empty their tanks (or whatever it is called) of that VCM gas. It has to be done, as far as I understand, by BURNING the remaining quantities, which takes some time. It seems that during the last night's bombing there were STILL some quantities of VCM in the tanks which were hit. The firemen went to put out the fire in all of the plants except the petrochemical ones, since it seems that it's safer if the gas is left to burn in the fire. The wind was blowing in the direction of the Danube, and again the people from the town were lucky. Until the early morning, at about 3AM, when the wind changed direction, and blew the smoke in the direction of the centre of town. At that point firemen were headed to the petrochemical plants.

Gordana and I decided to stay at home and watch the development of the situation. After some time we went to bed, with the radio on. I had strangely vivid dreams, for the first time since the strikes began. Not very interesting dreams, though, mostly just nonsense. Gordana and I were siting in a bar with friends, and members of The Rolling Stones were there as well. I was never a huge fan of the group (except for the earliest material), but I tried to sound friendly, and so did they.

When we woke up, one part of the town was covered with a white mist. The other part was covered with dark grey, black cloud coming from the oil refinery, which is still burning. The black cloud was up above the ground level, heading its way to the place where my parents live. They don't have a phone in their house, so I will have to go and visit them later today.

The mayor of Pancevo appeared on TV and said that the situation was not alarming at that moment, but is still far from normal. He asked people to stay in their houses and to follow the news. He also said that this was an obvious attempt to kill the town. He mentioned that at the beginning of the raids there were regular trains with cargo containing toxic material, travelling from Romania to Turkey, and it was again a mere coincidence that a huge catastrophe was not produced.

They said on the radio that four firemen were taken to hospital, because of smoke poisoning. Also, some of the workers from the industrial zone were injured.
Bye now Sasa

There was an announcement by an expert, who said that they were measuring the toxic levels in Pancevo since the beginning of the bombing last night. In the town area, the degree of toxicity was dependent of the direction of the wind. At 4 and 5AM, they said that the quantity of Vinyl Chloride Monomer gas, in some parts of the town, was about 7200 times greater than allowed by international standards! He also said that, as far as they know, this is the first time that such a quantity of that gas has poured out into a human settlement, and that petrochemical and artificial fertilizer plants had not been bombed in wars so far.

Another report said that around 50 people were poisoned, but the information is very scarce. Today we were riding our bikes, and we were watching the enormous black smoke coming out of the refinery, and spreading over town. Still, while I'm writing this, a huge flame is coming out from several plants at the refinery, 18 hours after the bombing.
Until soon Sasa

BLACK CLOUD
Mon, 19 Apr 1999 23:28:41

Hello! I am still trying to forget the "big blast" over Pancevo, two nights agp. It is reported that it was seen in town of Cacak, which is 200 km from here. And the nearest plant which was bombed could only be about 700 metres from our home. Can you imagine all those bombs, thrown on several industrial plants (with explosive materials etc.) exploding at the same time?

By the way, the oil refinery is still burning, two days after bombing. I can see the flame tall as a building. And the big black cloud of smoke coming out of it.

Yesterday, the black smoke was enormous, visible in Belgrade (about 17 km from Pancevo) as well. It must have been several kilometres long; we

A photograph taken from Sasa's flat

tried to make a photo, but it wasn't possible without some moving panoramic camera or something like that.

Gordana and I went to a grave yard, which must be some 4 or 5 kilometres from the refinery, and we were able to see the layers of soot on the surface of tomb-stones. At the same location, I saw a small white object falling from the sky. At first I thought that it could be a so-called "locator", a pocket radio device launched from NATO aircraft, which serves in the process of navigation of missiles (I think I told you I don't know too much about those things). It usually has a small parachute as well, and these devices are very often found in the fields around town.

Anyway, when I came closer to observe the thing, it turned out to be a piece of foam, which probably was carried by the wind all the way from oil refinery. Firemen were using foam to control the fire.

Yesterday, they were also getting rid of unexploded bombs at some location near Belgrade. There were many cases of unexploded missiles, found in the most bizarre places.

Speaking of bizarre, one of the most peculiar cases happened two nights ago, during the bombing of Batajnica, near Belgrade. After the bomb exploded, it launched small metal pieces hurting five people, and one piece crashed through the small window of the bathroom in a near-by house, and killed a three year old girl inside! Until next time, Sasa

April 20th Wed, 21 Apr 1999 05:41:28

Hello everybody! It was a nice sunny day yesterday, which – as we learned – is very suitable weather for bombing. I was trying not to think about it, and to relax my mind somehow, and I listened to my good old Bonzo Dog Band records for several hours, and did some drawing. But just in the early evening hours, the sky was getting cloudy, and – at least in this part of the country – the night was unusually quiet.

Still, the city of Nis, in the Southern part of Serbia, was a target of NATO strikes, with the tobacco plant almost totally destroyed. Some projectiles fell in the suburban area of the city as well, where the poor people dwell.

As of Pancevo, soon after the whole mess with the toxic material was over (or is it?!?!), it was discovered that there is another danger – this time the explosive material which still remained in the petrochemical complex. People from the parts of the town closest to the petrochemical plant were now warned to move during air raids to safer places, and the buses are taking them away to schools and sports centres. Our apartment building is right on the edge between the "dangerous" and "more safe" area. Also, everyone from the "danger" zone was warned not to eat food from their gardens, etc., before it is tested by experts.

I read about some people from the forest area, who spotted an unexploded NATO missile in the wasteland. By mere coincidence, when they were searching the ground around the projectile, the locals found the remains of the parts of an old cannon (probably from WW2)! There were pictures of them with two "weapons", old and new, suddenly appearing for the attention of the people from distant areas.

There was another story about a man from the town of Kursumlija, who – instead of joining his family in their basement shelter, had decided to remain sleeping in his bed during the air raids. For some reason, a NATO projectile fell on a near-by empty shack, causing a large explosion, and a 20 metre long crater. The house was almost totally destroyed, and part of the ceiling fell down, but the elderly man remained unhurt, lying in his bed. "I just opened my eyes, and saw the starry sky instead of the ceiling" – he said later. What's next? Bye Sasa

More, more about bombs
Wed, 21 Apr 1999 23:59:08

Hello folks The other day I watched my old video tapes of classic animated cartoons, mostly from the 40s. Beautiful, masterful shorts done by Tex Avery, Bob Clampett, etc. I have always been puzzled by the fact that some of the craziest, funniest ever cartoons were produced exactly during one of the bleakest moments in the history of the human kind, that was the Second World War. But now, during the big turmoil in my country at the end of the 20th century, I can understand that the very bleakness of the situation is producing a great need for humor, and perhaps it is a natural reaction, maybe it is just the level for our psyche to use our last reserves of vitality in these periods of crisis. Or maybe I'm wrong completely, as most of the people that I know are simply sad and melancholic, and feel so small and helpless.

Early in the morning NATO bombed a tower block in Belgrade, where some of the most outrageous, kitchy Serbian Television studios were based, along with the headquarters of the Milosevic's party, etc. I admit! I admit! – I was one who had a vivid fantasies about throwing a bomb on that same building, millions of times. But now that I saw an ACTUAL bomb (three of them!) being thrown, I can understand how stupid I was. Because, folks, IT IS ONLY A BUILDING! The BUILDING is nothing but a building, and if you bomb an office, just because you disagree with the policy of the people who worked there, you can be sure that: 1) you are dumb, and 2) you haven't solved the problem, my friend.

One of the first to protest against this meaningless act was the Serbian Independent Journalist Alliance, people from the independent media, who were spending the years being under the pressure of the very same people who were walking through the offices of that tower block.

Another "glorious" NATO action for today was the bombing of the only remaining bridge in the city of Novi Sad. The projectile left a big hole in the bridge construction. Novi Sad is the capital of the northern Serbian province of Vojvodina, a place with a very rich cultural and sub-cultural scene, a peaceful, multi-ethnic city that I always loved to visit.

Finally, speaking of bombs, here's a story about one which fell near the village Ribnica, in Southern Serbia, seriously injuring two civilians. The bomb contained a hand-written "message" by its sender: "Bad times. Isn't it lovely. See you guys. I'm going home, Eric N., Italy". Beside the serial number of the NATO bomb, which was 30003 70 4 AS 4829 MFP 96214 (AP). The bomb wounded the local farmer, and his 16-year old daughter, who received major skull fractures and is in a critical condition. See you soon. Sasa

The funny detail
Fri, 23 Apr 1999 00:47:22

Hello, just like many times before, Gordana bought a dozen eggs, from the woman who owns a small chicken farm, in a near-by village. When she brought the eggs home, we saw that they were unusually small in size. Later we found out that hens were disturbed by the numerous detonations (the farm is about 200 metres from some of the plants which were bombed!), and were starting to lay much smaller eggs. Such a funny little detail.

They said that, since the NATO strikes have destroyed numerous industrial plants, about 10 000 workers will be jobless, in my town alone. Not to mention the fact that to build an oil refinery takes several years, if you have the money to pay for it, of course. The whole community was very much dependent on the very industrial plants that were destroyed during the bombings, while the rest of the industry was already destroyed by the years of sanctions. Not to mention the fact that more than 20 bridges all over the country were ruined, as well as other important resources and the industrial and communication infrastructure, hardly anything to do with the military at all. Poor and bewildered people will become even more mad and will definitely act even more irrationally, and then they get a new ration of bombs sent from the angels hovering in the night sky above, and the civilized world will discover more and more good reasons to destroy the savage race that I belong to.

Strange things are happening with the snail mail sent to Serbia. I have received a couple of letters from Italy and US, with a delay though, but I know that some of the letters sent are either very late, or will not come at all. I was also informed that some post offices in UK and US are not accepting any mail to Serbia. Kjartan Arnorsson, a cartoonist from Iceland, has sent a small letter, and it was returned after a while, with a note in Danish, saying that mail deliveries to Serbia were cut off for now. A similar thing happened to a letter from a Russian cartoonist living in Berlin, Ilya Kitup. The letter was returned, and Ilya has forwarded his messages through a friend with access to email, saying – "I didn't insert any bombs for the Serbian army, and no strategic maps were enclosed". This is really funny, as I heard that even during WW2 the passage of mail was not interrupted. (Yeah. Too many comparisons with WW2 in my letters, I know). During the sanctions against Serbia, one of the meaningless measures was to restrict mail to Serbia as well. These measures are really stupid, if you realize that these days most information travels via internet, fax machines and telephones, etc. Snail mail has always been a symbol of intimate exchange of thoughts and ideas between people, and to cut it off is an anti-civilizational act, even if it's coming from the headquarters of the "civilized world". What do they think, that Serbia consists of 11 million clones of President Milosevic?

Lee Kennedy has been trying to send me a video tape with new Simpsons episodes, unsuccessfully. Damn it! Somebody from NATO has probably found out about our little conspiracy. The thing is, during the day, Miss Kennedy works as a humble telephone operator in an Opera house in London, and in her spare time she draws comics. During the night, she runs her own top-secret animation studio, where important codes and classified information has been implanted into the form of deceptively innocent sequences from funny animated cartoon series. When they get to Pancevo, they're decoded and used by the Serbian anti-aircraft defences, in order to destroy invisible NATO bombers.

And just as I write this, I'm listening to the news on the radio, about NATO bombs landing on downtown Uzice, near the post office (I still don't have the information if that was the original target, though). In Kosovo, they already have torn to pieces some post offices, of course. Oh, well. Bye Sasa

More destruction
Fri, 23 Apr 1999 23:01:02

Hello! Last night, around 2AM, Gordana and I were woken by the eerie sound of aircraft. Soon we heard distant, but very powerful explosions. Later we found out that it was probably a detonation caused by NATO projectiles which fell some 20 km from our home, at the offices of Serbian Television in Belgrade, while they were broadcasting news. The next morning we were disgusted to hear about this awful event! It was reported that at least ten people were killed, many were injured, and the rescue teams are still trying to find people under the ruins, who are officially considered as "missing". This was another horrible act by our friends from NATO, who officially announced just a few days ago that TV stations would not be considered as targets. The most stupid thing is that the people who were inside the building were mostly watchmen and the TV technicians! I phoned a friend who works as a film editor at Serbian TV (she was not on a duty during the bombing), and she was deeply shocked, and angry, because the technical crew consisted mostly of professionals, who were just doing their job. I myself have met and knew many people working or freelancing on TV, as I used to do freelance journalism for the art show on Channel 2 of national TV, called "The Nineties". I have been mostly working on short broadcasts on comics, presenting the works by cartoonists like Robert Crumb, Jim Woodring, Julie Doucet, Stefano Ricci and many others. The freelance job at the TV was not very well paid, and they still owe me money, but to BOMB a TV building, with people working inside, I tell you it's a horrible, sick idea. It is true that Serbian TV has been broadcasting (sometimes really ridiculous) government-instrumented propaganda for years, but it was mostly connected with the activities of the journalists and editors working for the "News/Information Staff". I think that most of the crew working in other fields were really competent, hard-working people – directors, producers, journalists, artists – people who didn't have much (if anything) to do with the notorious TV Newsreel!!! Programmes on culture, art, entertainment, drama, or education, were very solid.

The bombing of the TV building in the very heart of Belgrade has also caused damages to a near-by Russian Orthodox Church, and the building of the Childrens' Theatre! During the same strike, some of the power installations in Belgrade were destroyed, and many parts of the town were left in darkness. Yesterday, as I described before, NATO bombed the post office in the town of Uzice, and destroyed most of the phone lines. Today the central post offices in Pancevo was closed down, for security reasons. I will try to send these messages as long as I can, but I want you to know that this whole bombing thing is a dirty, murderous business! While we are getting close to entering the "twilight zone", please send all my compliments to the gentlemen celebrating NATO's 50th anniversary. Regards Sasa

```
Forwarded message
Fri, 23 Apr 1999 23:42:27
```

Here's the message I'm forwarding directly from the *Truth in Media* email list. No comment needed. S.

*****

An Eyewitness Account of NATO Murders at Serb TV HQ

I live 100 metres (about 110 yards) away from the Serb TV headquarters. At 2:06AM, we were sitting in our room, talking. Then we heard the awful sounds of a plane. It was so loud that we all hid under the bed, thinking that it would hit our building and kill us all.

Then we heard strong detonations. Our windows started rattling. The lights went out. We heard several more explosions. My neighbor, who is only 10 years old, fell down the stairs while trying to reach the shelter.

We were all panic-stricken because we heard strong detonations, and we thought that our building would fall apart. After that, we heard that Serb TV was hit. After some time, we went there to see what had happened. I can actually see the park (in front of the Serb TV building) from my window, but the building itself is behind some trees.

We saw smoke, fire, then we reached the building. Firemen, police, civil defense people were all already there trying to help the survivors.

We saw a woman shouting from the ruins: "Please, I am here, help me!!" Some men tried to get her out. She was walking around like a lunatic, shouting: "Where is Jelena? Jelena, she is still in the building!!"

Then we saw somebody falling from the second floor. We saw a man who was hanging upside down from the first, or second floor, I dunno. His head was all covered in blood. His legs were literally crushed by a concrete block. Everybody tried to help him. He is (or was) around 20–25 years old.

People were running around dripping with blood. Fire and smoke all over the place. Blood could be seen everywhere. A real massacre.

Then a friend of mine shouted "This man is dead!!" I didn't turn my head to see him because I thought I was about to faint. My friends went a bit further, and saw a corpse lying without a head. We also saw a pair of (woman's) legs lying crushed by another concrete block. I think that she was already dead, even though people tried to pull her out.

It was terrible. I don't know if I described it well enough. I am still shaking and I'm unable to think. People were lying wounded all over the place.

I can still smell the mixture of blood and smoke.

I hope you understand. All (Serb TV) buildings around were destroyed. I won't have any further comments on this. I'll need some more time to recover. That's all for now.

I also heard a reporter who was in the building saying: "The plane went really low, and then struck right at the entrance of the building."

This was not a crime against media, nor anything else NATO was claiming to save or prevent. This is a direct crime against humanity, and people the world over should know that. Thanks, Bob. Bye.

Marija Mitrovic, downtown Belgrade

*****

Adolf Hitler
Sun, 25 Apr 1999 00:28:36

Dear folks, I somehow lost my account of time. By the end of April, Gordana and I were supposed to go to Italy, to an exhibition called *Happening Underground*, in Milan. The exhibition will take place in Centro Sociale Leonkavalo (Centro Sociale is an Italian term for the squatted Youth Centre where different cultural activities take place). Of course, because of the war, I won't be allowed to go out of the country. And once when we will be free to go and see our friends abroad, God knows what our route will look like, as the roads, airports, and bridges in my country have been bombed, and there will be more destruction in the future.

Rescue teams are still trying to find the people under the ruins of Serbian TV, 40 hours after the bombing. They have found 6 more bodies in the recent hours, but there are some indications that some people trapped under walls are still alive.

In the news we hear about more and more NATO projectiles hitting Pristina, the capital of Kosovo. More and more bombs landing on the towns in the South of Serbia. The cloudy weather is probably our only protector from more bombs falling from the sky, instead of the rain, which is now tipping on my window. Ha ha, I'm getting into a poetic mood.

The other day I was thinking about the fact that propaganda on all sides is trying to compare their "enemies" to the Nazis, and the enemy leader is too often marked as a new "Adolf Hitler". It just reflects the old "black and white" concepts, which are still in life on all sides! It seems that, for the people of the 20th century, Hitler is a substitute for old religious beliefs in Satan, as the root of all evil. The end justifies the means, and if you call somebody "Hitler", it means that you have the right to kill him, or burn his town, torture his dog, or whatever, and still call yourself a saint.

The Allies' bombings and destruction of the towns in Germany during the WW2, and the A-bombs thrown on the cities of Japan, brought just as much suffering to the innocent people, as the unthinkable crimes by the Nazi system. We are obviously still living in a world where conflicts are being resolved almost exclusively by bombs or by using brute force. We are a sick, savage civilization, hiding behind big words and ugly faces of the administration. If there was anything that shows up from this recent war in my country, it is that, at the end of the 20th century, the system is still stronger than people who populate it. The victims of this conflict are small, common people, no matter if they are Serbs, Albanians, or soldiers from NATO countries. And at the same time, all the crimes were done IN THEIR NAME, and all the crimes were projected and triggered by a system. It is the system that is sick, not people.
Regards Sasa

Zero
Sun, 25 Apr 1999 21:06:03

Hello No message today. Maybe tomorrow.
Bye Sasa

I'm Back!!!
Tue, 4 May 1999 10:30:13

Yes, we are OK. I will have to write this very fast because we have the power at the moment, but no one is sure how long it will last. Yesterday, after another NATO bombing, almost the whole Serbia was left without electricity (and without running water, as well, it is all connected). We have both power and water at the moment, in this part of the town at least, but I don't know how long it will last (they said probably a very short time), or if the same facilities will be bombed again soon. Last week, I left you without these "reports", simply because my computer was broken. It's a jinx. When finally a computer-keen friend of mine came to see it, it turned out that the hard disc was dead. I lost everything that was on it. Damn it. And had to buy a new (second-hand, though) hard disc too. Some 20 minutes after the hard disc was installed, there was the NATO bombing of the power plants, and I wasn't able to use the machine again.

Anyway, in the past week or so, Pancevo was bombed only a couple of times. One of the bombs fell in the centre of the town, in the park in front of the hospital. It was either a NATO mistake, or the projectile was hit by anti-aircraft defense (I still don't know). By coincidence or a miracle, two people (who were in the car, very close to the place where the bomb fell) survived the whole incident, even though the car was damaged. Two nearby newstands were detroyed, and there is a hole in the concrete down on the pavement, and broken trees in the park. The administrative part of the hospital was demolished, and – only some 50 metres away – there is a maternity hospital, where a woman gave birth to twins, just at the time of the explosion!

Some good friends of ours (Olivera and Rade) live in a house some 30 metres from the place that was bombed. They were inside the house when the whole thing happened, and they heard an awful noise, before their room was suddenly lit up, as if it was day, and not 1AM. Still, Olivera sounded happy when Gordana spoke to her – she was happy to be alive, after all. There were just minor damages to the house, luckily.

It is obvious that more and more civilian targets have been hit by NATO, including two of buses full of people in Kosovo, a horrifying scene. The other day, on a more lighter side, the guys connected to *Kulturbunt* fanzine from Pancevo, have organized a projection of 4 short video films, created during the past few weeks. The most interesting film consists of parts from the movie (1984) based on Orwell's novel, aired on the local TV, and interrupted by the sudden news about bombings of Pancevo, and the ecological problems that it produced. I'll try to post more messages as soon as it is possible. We are just trying to cook as much food as possible in a short time, prepare some coffee, etc. That's so prosaic, damn it.

Bye Sasa + Gordana

Ice cream in the dump
Thu, 6 May 1999 00:37:09

Hello everybody! Still, for many hours during the day, we are left without power and running water. As you can guess, it is really bad for the food supplies we stored in our refrigerators and freezers. I like to eat sweet things (like a baby!), and it breaks my heart to hear about the cake shop's supplies of ice cream that had to be thrown away at the dump, in the midst of the crisis. As I mentioned before, Belgrade's zoo is placed within the remains of the city's old fortification, pretty close to the main pedestrianised street, called Knez Mihajlova. The people who run the zoo were trying to solve the problem of large and dangerous animals running away from the zoo, in case the fortification was bombed. So during the air raids, there is a gun squad that comes to the zoo, ready to shoot the animals. First they were thinking about putting the animals to sleep, but the serum lasts just for several hours, and nobody knows what might happen in the duration of a bombing (as was the case in World War 2, when wild animals were running all over the streets of Belgrade, together with people bewildered by "carpet bombing").

Speaking of bombings, they are still finding the bodies under the ruins in a small town of Surdulica, a week after NATO had bombed a civilian block of houses. It was a horrible event, with most of the victims being children, hiding in a shelter. The bodies were torn to pieces, and it was very hard to identify them. It was reported that two more people committed suicide, after this event. Recently, I spoke to a friend from a little town in Southern Serbia. He was trying to do something for the local scene for years, and organized several comics and panel cartoon exhibitions in the town. As the war began, he was (together with other friends, Serbs as well) involved in helping a family who escaped from Kosovo. The family that fled from Pristina consists of an Iraqi man (a political immigrant who has already fled from his homeland in the 80s, who studied and found a job in Kosovo), an Albanian woman, and two of their children. They said that nobody had kicked them out of their homes, but the situation was so dramatic, that everybody was already terrified and afraid of the Serbian paramilitary groups which were seen all over town, and NATO bombings (one of the first targets was a mail office in Pristina, which left everyone, Serbs and Albanians, without phone lines), and the overall chaos that prevailed. Some of their friends helped them to escape from Kosovo to a nearby town in Southern Serbia, where my friend let them stay in his house until they were able to recover. They decided to leave for Algeria, which is also a country with lots of problems, but they had some friends and possibilities for a job out there. According to the information that I heard on Radio Free Europe, the number of the Serbs fleeing from Kosovo is, proportionally, even bigger than the number of Albanians. Everybody seems to running away from the place, except for the men in uniforms, and that is so frightening. OK, I'm trying to send this before another black-out. Regards Sasa

No escape
Thu, 6 May 1999 15:06:13

Hello! Just spoke to my cousins who (shortly after the NATO strikes against Pancevo industrial zone have started) moved to their parents' house in the village of Dubovac, on the banks of the Danube. It is a fishing settlement, not so faraway from the Romanian border, and it was very quiet there, and good for the children – who are not going to school anyway, and mostly get sick after hiding in the basement shelters. Anyway, life in Dubovac was much better then living in our targeted industrial town, but not for long. Soon after Romania recently gave permission to NATO planes to fly over that country's territory, the sound of the aircraft was audible even over the picturesque village, together with the "spectacular" fire from anti-aircraft defenses – firing both from the ground and from the ships on Danube. The army was quickly moving from place to place in order to escape NATO counter-attacks. There was also some guy, coming to my cousin's neighborhood, who is an amateur radio operator – joining the web that spread all over country, which enabled a very effective exchange of information about the casualties, bombings, or the direction where the NATO aircraft were heading. Soon the life in Dubovac has begun to resemble too much like a war movie, and my cousins decided to go back to town, saying that it was getting harder and harder to escape from this madness anyway!

Yes, the war came to many small towns and villages in the countryside, around the whole territory of the country. We heard about the the guy from Pancevo, who also went to a peaceful village in the countryside, where he felt quite relaxed, until the day when something fell right into his backyard – it turned out to be a NATO aircraft fuel reservoir!! (Those reservoirs are very often dropped from their planes, but I don't know the reasons why). One of the puzzling thing about the bombing, especially when connected to bridges, is that sometimes it is really hard to understand the reasons or plans behind these actions. A town in central Serbia, called Trstenik, is a place where my father was born. This peaceful little town seemed to be away from the bombing "schedule", until just recently, when NATO aircraft dropped bombs on a small bridge in the very centre of Trstenik, killing a woman who was passing the bridge on her bicycle. Everybody was appalled, because the bridge was very old, surrounded by shops and civil houses, and mostly used by pedestrians – it was too small to allow any sort of traffic of heavy vehicles, or anything like that. To make things more absurd, the same little bridge was bombed twice more, until it was torn to pieces. Well, it's all hard to understand, folks, but that's the reality that so many people here have to face somehow.

Bye Sasa

May 7th 1999

Hello!! Well, on the top of everything, yours truly has been "flying" today -- it was a short "flight", but spectacular (ha ha!). Yes, I had an accident, while riding a bicycle, and my left hand is in plaster, I broke my elbow, damn it. It's good that it was my LEFT hand that was hurt, otherwise I would not be able to draw. I was riding my bicycle, heading to the Gallery of Contemporary Arts, in the centre of the town, where there was an opening of the exhibition of work by 20 young and alternative artists from the town, who were showing their pieces created during the NATO attacks, and one of my strips was on display as well. As most of the strikes are being executed during the late evening, the opening was held at 1PM.

Anyway, I was riding past the cars parked on the road, and a soldier who was in a car opened his door without looking back first, and I crashed into it, and was "launched" about two metres ahead, and it was a wonder that my bike was in one piece after all, just with the forks slightly deformed. The guy said that he was sorry, and I said "OK", and after seeing that I was in one piece, I just wanted to get out of the place, to hide from the embarrassment, because everybody was looking at my "pirouette" and the bicycle laying on the ground, right in the centre of town.

Just a couple of hours before this, NATO bombed the very centre of the city of Nis, in Southern Serbia, and at least 15 people were killed and about 60 were injured. A friend from Prokuplje (small town near Nis) phoned and told me about one woman from his town who was in the final stage of pregnancy, and went to a maternity hospital in Nis. She was killed while passing through the market near the place which was bombed. The scenes from Nis looked apocalyptic. Dead people on the pavements, smoke, burning cars, ruined shops and civilian houses. The hospital was badly damaged, the mortuary and pathology ward were hit. Cluster bombs were found all over the centre of the city – they are designed similar to soft drink cans.

Today, while speaking to my parents, they told me a strange thing – during the first NATO bombing of the power lines, when they used some special weapon, never used before, to produce a black out over most of the territory of Serbia, my mother was in front of her house (they have a small orchard garden). She saw something that appeared like light balls moving on the power lines and rolling on the fields around. The power station is just a few hundred metres from my parents' home, and they would often look in the direction of it – as they feared that it was going to be bombed, but this time there were no detonations at all. It seems that what my mother saw were the "soft bombs", a new product made in the NATO laboratories. It seemed so funny to think about my parents witnessing the world-premiere of a new weapon.

Remember that I mentioned the NATO aircraft fuel pods falling all over the country? One was found today, at the plantation where Gordana works. The man who was riding a tractor there found a large crater in the middle of the field, and went to the police to report it. After the experts come to the site, they found a dropped fuel pod, but it's still not clear WHEN it fell down. While reading the newspapers, you can find a lot of war horror stories – two days ago, they have found a body of a 6 year old boy, floating in the river. He was identified as one of the victims from the train which was bombed by NATO three weeks ago.

May 8th 1999

Last night, I hardly had any rest, because of the pain in my elbow, and the problems of learning to put my plastered hand in the most comfortable position while trying to sleep. Not to mention new techniques that I was trying to develop, like – how to put in contact lenses singlehanded.

Our window panes were trembling because of the strong detonations coming from the direction of Belgrade. NATO first used their "soft bombs" during the evening, to short out the electrical lines. After that, while still in the dark, many parts of the city were exposed to heavy bombing, in four strikes, the last of which took place in the early morning hours Some of the streets in the centre were closed down, with broken glass and pieces of concrete and pieces of shrapnel all over the place. One of the buildings that was bombed was, to everybody's surprise, the Chinese Embassy! Two projectiles hit the building, killing 3 people (thus far) including a Chinese journalist, and injuring more people.

Until soon Sasa

NO COMMUNICATION
Sun, 9 May 1999 22:51:14

Hello friends! Last night, a main post office in Kragujevac, in Central Serbia, was hit by a NATO bomb, but it didn't explode. During the same night, another post office – in a town of Uzice, was completely destroyed by NATO projectiles, and in a second attack, the same building – which was already in ruins – was bombed once more. The whole area was left without phone connections. The same thing could happen here in my town as well, and it makes me sad to think that we could be cut off from our friends all over the world. By the way, I have found more funny NATO leaflets – they are so collectible! I've already gathered an interesting collection. The newest one is with the target sign (so, it seems that – eventually – it was adopted even by NATO designers!) and with the message: NO FUEL, NO POWER, NO TRADE, NO FREEDOM, NO FUTURE: MILOSEVIC. Milosevic's photo (a rather small one) is also included.

Could these leaflets, dropped (maybe?) from the same planes that are dropping bombs on the towns below, be meaningful media for communication with the Serbian people? Ironically, one of the small TV stations here aired the *Mars Attacks* movie few weeks ago. One of the scenes includes Martians destroying the towns and people of the Earth, while at the same time there was a voice from their speaker saying (with a "Martian" accent): "DON'T RUN AWAY! WE ARE YOUR FRIENDS! I REPEAT: DON'T RUN AWAY! WE ARE YOUR FRIENDS!!"

This whole situation seemed strangely familiar to what we are experiencing in this silly land of Serbia. Anyway, after most of the offices and the transmitters of the major TV stations (some of which were owned by the state, and some which were private ones) in Serbia were rocketed, in some parts of the country you can see only a couple of programs, aired by some small local transmitters, but in some parts there is no signal of any TV station left. Instead, I heard that some people were able to receive the signal of some sort of NATO TV program, in the Serbo-Croat language, transmitted probably from nearby countries. I wasn't able to watch any of it, but I can guess that most of the people here will not be delighted to watch a program with a NATO trademark, after the domestic stations have been blown to pieces by the very same organization (even though most of the Serbian stations were mostly airing American movies and TV series anyway. At the beginning of the bombing campaign, as I described, there were some attempts by local censors to exclude American movies and series from the Serbian media. But it lasted just a few days or so).

It is obvious that war kills communication, and that people who are pointing weapons of destruction at each other don't really want to establish meaningful communication in the first place. I should say again, and again, that we are living in a savage world, hiding behind the happy face of mass communication. We are still learning to talk to each other. And we've almost forgotten that it is a simple and natural thing to do. Bye bye Sasa

Broken glass on the pavement
Tue, 11 May 1999 23:42:05

Hello!! Yesterday I walked through Kneza Milosa street in Belgrade, right in the centre of the town. Many buildings in this and the surrounding streets were destroyed by NATO bombs – it is the part of the town where many government and military HQ buildings are placed, together with foreign embassies, etc. One of the bombs that fell hadn't exploded, and was activated recently, in the middle of the day, causing more damage and destruction. Broken glass and heavy blocks of bricks and mortar were launched all around, and a few streets were closed to traffic. I've read an article about a small town in Belgium, which is also called Belgrade, where they even have a football club called Red Star! "I hope that they will not bomb us by mistake" – said one of the citizens of Belgrade, Belgium, referring to many NATO "mistake bombings". By the way, there are at least 3 or 4 Belgrades in the USA as well.

Last night one of the army barracks in Pancevo (placed near the train station) was bombed by NATO. Barracks were already emptied, but the detonation damaged many civilian houses in town. Today, at about 2PM, anti-aircraft defenses in villages around Pancevo were bombed after a sudden NATO attack, and several villagers were injured, with their houses and goods seriously damaged. A friend of ours, who plays drums in a band called NUP, and is one of the cartoonists gathered around my "kitchen" comics workshop, was drafted into a defense unit placed in his native village of Banatsko Novo Selo. We tried to call and see if he was OK, but the lines were busy all the time, probably because so many people were calling their friends and relatives. Djavo (the drummer) called me later, and said that he was on a vacation during that attack, thank god.

Today, while I drew my new comic strip, I played a lot of Jonathan Richman's records. A couple of months ago, together with a guy from the B92 radio station, I was trying to contact Jonathan and convince him to play in Belgrade, after his concert in Salonika, in Greece, planned for mid March. It turned out that Jonathan's schedule was too busy, and he missed the opportunity to play in Serbia some days before the bombing, ha ha. More detonations around Pancevo while I write this. The sound of detonations is something that we will not forget, even when the war is over. It echoes inside your psychological structure, and I'm sure that it will come up in my dreams for many years to come. Until soon S.

FAREWELL?
Thu, 13 May 1999 10:31:51

This may or may not be a farewell, but we are forwarding a message that we received from Charles Alverson this morning. If you don't hear from us, we send you our love and will write just as soon as possible. If you have any urgent message, send it straight away before the black out, even if I might not be able to answer. We still hope that they will not be so stupid to shut down the internet. Maybe they will change their mind or something.

Regards, Sasa and Gordana

★★★★★

Dear Friends, relations, extortion victims: I just (Thursday morning, 13/5/99) received the following. If you suddenly (or slowly) don't hear from me, this might well be the reason. Or it might just be a bit of wartime paranoia. All best, Charles Alverson

Subject: US shuts down Yugoslav Internet – For immediate release

Dear sirs, We have reliable information that the US Government ordered the Loral Orion company to shut down its satellite feeds for Internet customers in Yugoslavia. This action may be taken as soon as later tonight or tomorrow (May 12 or 13, 1999). This is a flagrant violation of commercial contracts with Yugoslav ISPs, as well as an attack on freedom of the Internet. A web site in protest of these actions should be up shortly. We will supply you with the URL. In the meantime, please be so kind to inform as many people as possible about this tragic event for the Internet community in Yugoslavia and Europe.

Kind regards, BeoNET Belgrade, Yugoslavia

★★★★★

The sound of a fighter plane
Thu, 13 May 1999 00:48:40

Hello folks It turned out that yesterday, around 2PM, during the NATO bombing of the anti-aircraft defenses placed near the villages around Pancevo, a bus was passing just about 30–40 metres from the place where the bombs fell. It is the same bus that Gordana takes every day when she goes to work, and today she spoke to the bus conductor who witnessed the whole event. The conductor said that people in the bus heard the sound of planes, and the next thing they saw were bombs exploding near a house on the side of the road, while military vehicles were passing it (they are forced to constantly move their anti-aircraft weaponry), heading to a near-by forest. Not only that the house was crushed and set on fire, but the explosion launched parts of the construction all around. One of the bricks hit and broke the window of the bus, but, by a wonder, none of the passengers were hurt. Everybody was appalled! The bus stopped, and didn't continued its ride before some time had passed, as all needed to collect their mind. Three of the villagers were injured, including the poor older couple from the house that was completely demolished. I was thinking that one of the most terrorizing aspects of this bombing campaign is that it is actually so wide, that no one knows if the house on the end of the road is going to be torn to pieces, or whether some peaceful neighbor is in danger of being targeted, or what is going to happen next. And still, the whole action is presented as "selective" as if projected to be human and civilized.

War, any war, is built on the idea of destruction, which mostly means just killing. To innocent people who have died or been injured or left homeless, it hardly matters if their executors were Milosevic's brutal special forces, or fanatics from the KLA, or NATO's sophisticated machinery. The final result is always the same: innocent people that are bleeding. If this is covered with the facade of "civilized behaviour" and "progress" embodied in the shiny machines of modern technology, it makes it only more frightening.

As for the sound of NATO aircraft, which is everybody's nightmare here, I received a letter by a friend from San Francisco, the cartoonist Chris Lanier: "Here in San Francisco", said Chris, "every year they have an event called 'Fleet Week'. It has something to do with the Navy, I don't know what. A lot of gunboats shore up in the harbor, and various fighter planes put on a spectacle of formation flying above the bay. The 'Blue Angels' always fly, doing loops, leaving vapor trails in the sky. The week before the performance is terrible. The fighters fly their test runs, zooming over the neighborhoods, rattling the windows, shaking the ground, thrumming the eardrums with the roar of their engines. The news always does something about the 'Blue Angels', showing footage of them arcing through the air, the sun photogenically glinting from their steel blue wings. I think it never occurs to the majority of the spectators at Fleet Week that what they are watching are not machines built to entertain them – machines built to do loop-de-loops and make vapor-trail geometric designs – but rather machines that were built for the sole purpose of slaughtering people. I don't think that most people here realize that the sound of fighter plane engines, for most people in the world, is a sound that causes terror, that announces the proximity of the bombs. They just hear it as the sound of Fleet Week".

Bye Sasa

Internet war and peace
Sat, 15 May 1999 21:31:35

Hello people! YES! We still have access to the Internet. Despite that, New York's Loral Space and Communications company (which deals with the US communication satellites business), said that they may be forced to cut internet access to Serbia, it seems that this decision has been withdrawn for the moment. I don't pretend that I understand how this all operates, but anyway Yugoslav providers have announced yesterday that they will be able to find alternative Internet links, even if they will be cut off from access to satellites. Still, Serbian Internet users are having difficulties because of the NATO "soft bombs" used against power lines, and frequent black outs, etc., not to mention the bombing of the communication infrastructure.

Recently I received a warning note, because many Internet users in Serbia have received a computer virus through a file attachment titled "Stop the bombing". Many think that the virus was probably produced in NATO countries, or maybe even by somebody directly connected to NATO, as the design is obviously made to attract the Internet users who are opposed to bombing. Anyway, the Internet has had an important impact on this war, as it has provided a communication link between people, even if their governments are at war, and it may be an important tool for the future peace process of this sick world we're living in. Two nights ago, NATO switched out the electricity in many towns in Serbia. During last night, black outs were caused not by NATO bombs, but by a storm. As in a few occasions before, everybody was trying to distinguish the thunder and lightning from bomb blasts (which is not easy). Several times during this bombing campaign there were earthquakes shaking Serbian soil as well, and, like many others, I haven't even noticed it, in the midst of all the explosions.

Yesterday, the number one news was the NATO bombing of another Albanian refugee column, in a village of Korisa, in Kosovo. As I write this, more then 80 people, mostly women and children, were found dead!!! A shocking sight that we have seen already too often in this war, when powerful NATO projectiles have exploded too close to unprotected people: remains of human flesh torn to pieces. According to a report (a few days old) among about 300 civilians who were killed by NATO bombs thrown at the territory of Kosovo, about half were Albanians. The misery was equally distributed, among the nations in this meaningless conflict.

The whole Kosovo is radiating a vibration of violence and despair. Yesterday I spoke to a friend who lives in a small town in Southern Serbia. A town that is very close to Kosovo, and my friend could often see the endless series of blasts, echoes of the countless NATO bombings coming from that direction. What is also visible is traffic of buses adjusted for transportation of injured Serbian soldiers. As it is not possible to transport all the wounded people by regular ambulances, they have taken out the seats from buses, and inserted beds instead. A large number of injured people can be transported that way. A friend has told me that he spoke to a man who is a driver of another type of vehicle, a military car which transports dead soldiers from Kosovo to the city of Nis. The man was almost mad from misery. On top of his morbid "everyday activity", while he was passing through the periphery of some village in Kosovo, by chance he spotted a man who, looking from a distance, seemed to be kneeling down underneath the branches of the trees. It turned out that it was a body of a man who committed suicide. Later they found that it was an Albanian who was overwhelmed by despair and hanged himself. "It was a small, tiny tree, and it must have been the enormous urge to die which enabled that man to actually kill himself" – said the driver, whispering to my friend.

Bye Sasa

Earthquakes, storms and bombs
Mon, 17 May 1999 23:35:14

Hello to everybody! Today, again, central Serbia was shaken both by an earthquake, and by NATO bombs. The earthquake was not as strong as the one which happened just a few days ago, but last Friday was marked by another catastrophe caused by nature, not by man: a heavy storm that destroyed many crops in Northern Serbia – some fruit trees will not be ready for harvest for several years. In some parts, they reported pieces of ice 5–6 cm large falling from the sky, and destroying rooves and parked cars. The damage made to some towns was not very different from the damage caused by NATO bombs!!

Today, one of the NATO targets was again the highway route from Belgrade to Nis. One of the bombs fell but didn't explode, and it was just another way to (unintentionally, though) disrupt the traffic in that part of the road. A railroad near the same spot (Velika Plana) was also destroyed by NATO projectiles. Gordana and I travel down that highway every summer, when we go to my parents' cottage in a place called Gamzigrad. We go on vacation there, but I also go to search for the fossils hidden in the rocks around the place. Gamzigrad was always inspirational for my dream explorations as well – it was in Gamzigrad, years ago, that I had vivid dreams about cartoons, which inspired me to start developing the idea of dream comics. This year, it will probably take much more time to reach the place, and God knows if this summer we will be able to think about vacation at all, as our concerns may be much more concentrated on the invasion of NATO ground troops! Some reality we are inhabiting!

Saw a TV report about a NATO pilotless aircraft (owned by the German airforce) which was hit by anti-aircraft defenses. Few of the aircraft of this type have been shot down thus far. There was even a dramatic video report that shows a moment when one of those planes was crashing down. As these planes are used for observing targeted areas, it must be interesting to watch the material they filmed, as it was reported that in some of the aircraft the tape was found intact. One of the shocking things about the bombing of the column of Albanian refugees in the village of Korisa a few days ago, according to the Serbian media, is that NATO used "thermo bombs" – an awful weapon which produces a high temperature (about 2000 degrees Celsius!!), which explains the horrible, horrible pictures of burnt bodies found at the site. We thought that "soft bombs", constructed to switch out the power lines, were the last of the "new weapons" used in this war. But God knows what we may expect next. If the war continues to escalate, it will be a nice opportunity for someone to try everything they treasured in stocks of the military laboratories. OK, that's enough for today. Bye Sasa

Question from a dream
Tue, 18 May 1999 22:04:09

Hello! Today I received a letter by Bob Kathman, from Baltimore, with whom I co-edited *Flock of Dreamers*, an international anthology of dream-inspired comics, published last year by Kitchen Sink Press. I've been discussing dreams and comics with Bob for years. Here's the description of his most recent dream:

"I dreamt last night I was in Belgrade and I was travelling through it in a car with some people. I had a dread of bombing even though the streets were quiet. I thought 'It seems safe but here I am and who knows.' a bomb could fall at any time and since they are bombing the city, I could be in the way. I wonder if everyone thinks like this before actually being bombed?"

I was thinking about Bob's question from a dream. What do people actually think before or during the bombing? The only person that I met who was near the immediate place where the bomb fell, was Gordana's friend, a woman who was at her workplace during the bombing of the petrochemical plant in Pancevo. The whole working process was already switched to automatic handling, so her job was to control the production behind a monitor. When the bomb exploded, she was injured by the glass which fell on her. She described the whole experience as an enormous shock, stronger than the actual pain caused by the injury. She has been trying to collect her mind for days, but only later did she have a time to think how lucky she was because her monitor hadn't exploded! I remember that during the "big blast" in Pancevo, when all three plants in the industrial zone in town were bombed during a single attack, and toxic gases were freed, my mind was also in a state of shock. Just to see the enormous blast which turned night into a day was enough to shake your entire being. But I remember as well that there was a voice deep, deep inside me, which was telling me that everything is going to be all right. Today, by the way, there was an official humanitarian UN delegation, visiting the destroyed plants in the industrial zone in Pancevo. Ironically, during the time of the visit, one of the NATO projectiles fell in Obrenovac (Belgrade's suburbia), some 30 km away, destroying a private house. While leaving Pancevo, the UN delegation had a car accident, and two members of the mission were injured. As of my own activities, I just finished a fifth installment of my new strip, titled "Regards from Serbia". Yes, Chris Ware has convinced me to start working on a weekly strip. See you tomorrow Sasa

Dreams, prisons and graveyards
Wed, 19 May 1999 23:22:33

Hello! Hey, I'm glad that I keep on visiting my friends cartoonists in their dreams. Rick Veitch told me about his dream of me being happy because I got some grant, and it was true, in reality, to my own surprise! Just a few days before Rick dreamt this, I was informed that my grant for a trip to Seattle was accepted, and I'll go there for 6 weeks if the war stops before October ! Today I received a letter from Mack White, here's an excerpt:

"In your report this morning you described Bob's dream. Considering your interest in dreams, I thought you'd be interested in one I had last night. You were in it:

I dreamed I traveled to Serbia. The reason was because the Internet had been shut down and I needed to contact you. Someone was guiding me through a neighborhood to your home. For some reason we had to wait on a street corner for you to meet us. It was night and there was a weird red glow to everything.

While standing there, I took a walk down a river, or canal, which was full of refugees on rafts. All the refugees were carrying large plastic bottles of Coca-Cola. I remember thinking, 'I should follow their example and stock up on Coke for Y2K.'

I had wandered a bit far. So I headed back to the rendezvous point.

While we were waiting, an old man on a bicycle stopped to talk to my guide. Then a car appeared, and both of them ran off and hid. I was too slow, so didn't hide. I thought, 'I need to pay better attention to what's happening around me, or I'll get killed.'

The car passed. Inside were some men who fixed me in a menacing stare. I waited for them to start shooting, but they didn't. They just drove on past.

My guide reappeared from his hiding place. The wait continued. I went into a store and found copies of XL on sale. Inside was your comic strip. I bought three, intending to give one to you.

Then I went back to the street corner. About that time you appeared. You and I shook hands. You said you had some changes in the intro I had written(?!). Then we headed back to your home, which was a big building crowded with people. Everyone was tense.

You were busy doing something (setting up some musical instruments for a performance of some kind), but I insisted you stop for a moment so I could show you the newspaper which had your comic strip in it. When I picked up the stack of newspapers, they turned into sleeping bags. They were black.

I woke up. My girlfriend woke up at the same time, oddly. I told her about the dream. 'I'm worried,' I said. 'I think this is going to turn into a ground war.'

The reason I said that was because, thinking about the black sleeping bags in the dream, I remembered a report that was circulating several weeks ago that NATO had ordered several thousand body bags sent to their base of operations. Apparently, they have been anticipating a ground war from the start. So, that was the immediate association I made when I remembered the sleeping bags in the dream. A ground war".

Mack's dream reminded me of many talks that I had with friends here, who were all concerned about the possibility of a ground war, despite the efforts of the past few days to end this crisis in a diplomatic way (diplomacy mostly comes too late). Serbian soldiers in Kosovo were probably having similar thoughts on their mind while reading NATO leaflets – one of the pamphlets shows an Apache helicopter attacking a Serbian tank, with the warning: DON'T WAIT FOR ME! Today, a bizarre thing happened in a place called Istok, in Kosovo: NATO has bombed a local prison! Three projectiles hit prison cells in the central building, two prisoners were killed, one guard and some more prisoners were injured. But what is bizarre any more? In early April, NATO projectiles fell on the Serbian Orthodox Christian graveyard in Kosovo's capital. Reporters were astonished to see not only the tombstones demolished, but also coffins and human bones showing up from the 10 metres wide crater. Regards Sasa

Down on Earth
Fri, 21 May 1999 00:13:38

Hello to all! Yesterday, shortly before his visit to Serbia, Russia's official Victor Chernomidin said that he is coming to Belgrade to settle negotiations, even though his government has the information that various points of the city would be bombed by NATO the same evening. Shortly after his plane went back to Russia, there was a series of detonations coming from the direction of Belgrade. I was able to see very intense activity of the anti-aircraft defenses as well, and even the eerie flight of cruise missiles. All kind of detonations were audible for hours, and – for the first time, I even saw what I think was the launching of a projectile from an aircraft positioned somewhere up there in the sky. Among the results of last night's attacks was another case of a NATO projectile missing its target (as later admitted by NATO officials) that hit the Hospital in a part of town called Topcider! The direct hit ruined the "intensive care" ward at the Neurology Centre, killing three patients, and injuring more of them, as well as some medical workers. In one of the wards, an operation was still going on when the missile hit the building. Bloody sheets and smashed medical equipment all over the place, an urgent evacuation going on immediately after the bombing. Another drama.

All over Serbia, most of the patients who were not seriously ill have already been sent home, which means that those who were still left in the hospitals really needed medical care. Tonight, a few hours ago, NATO bombed a fuel tank in Belgrade. After detonation, glass broke in the windows of the near-by residency of the Swiss embassy, where there was a meeting being held, in honor of its country's Independence Day. One of the officials invited was the Swedish Ambassador. Ironically, it was the Swedish embassy that was damaged yesterday, during the bombing of the hospital in Topcider. Today, I spoke to a friend about the pilots of the aircraft who are sent to bomb our land. It really must be a hard job. I guess that every land, viewed from the air, looks beautiful, and the pilots have to drop bombs, right on the towns and people below, and risk their lives for some reason that is more or less abstract to them. In a way, they are the victims of this war, just like those tiny little people down on earth.

See you Sasa

Hello! Today there were many detonations coming from all directions. It's always bizarre when you hear the bombs exploding during a nice sunny day (even though a storm was raging in the evening). I saw the dogs down the street standing still, taking curious positions and looking in the direction of the NATO aircraft roar. I don't recall that they were so sensitive to the sound of the airplanes before the bombing campaign began. Today, even Banatski Brestovac, a village where Gordana goes to work, was added to the list of targeted areas! This almost sounds like a joke. Gordana was at the fruit plantation at work, when a detonation shook the ground – NATO had thrown a bomb in the fields where the anti-aircraft defenses were positioned (we don't even know if anybody was injured, as the military do not provide the information about army casualties). There were reports today about renewed NATO bombings of the prison in Istok, in Kosovo. This time the shelling was even more intense! At least 20 NATO projectiles were fired, which is a frightening number. And just as scary is the number of people killed (20), both prisoners and guards! When the strike was over, domestic and foreign journalists visited the place, but shortly after they went away, there was another strike and the prison was bombed again!!! They just said on the radio that from the morning until the evening, this target was struck six times!! I can't figure out the reasons behind this drastic action at the moment, and I wonder if the reports will capture the drama which must be happening there. Among the more bizarre targets there was a radio transmitter and a meteorological station in Subotica, bombed the other day. It was stupid that NATO has destroyed the transmitter, as it belongs to the local station Radio Subotica, which was always opposed to the state's radio propaganda. Or are they bombing just ANY transmitter they spot? And how about the meteorological station, more than 100 years old?! Were they producing tanks there?! This all looks like NATO do not have much targets left after 8 weeks of bombing of this poor and exhausted country, and now they bomb just anything.

Yes, it's 8 weeks of bombing already, and one of the things that I miss is the good old snail mail, and books and letters in my mail box. Thank god we've still got some other means of communication left, like the internet, or dreams. Plus I can express myself through my "cartoon" self in my comics, and that is definitely some sort of communication as well. Here's a letter from my friend Gaian from Italy:

"Last week I dreamt I was sleeping in my bed, in Bari, and I heard deep and low noises from out of the window. I opened the window, and I saw reddish lights on the horizon. Actually, I can see the sea from the window of my room, and on sunny days, when the sky is clear, it is possible to see the coast of Albania even without field-glasses. In my dream the landscape was the same, but the strip of land was not Albania, I don't know what it was. When I saw these lights at the horizon, I said: 'Sasha, what is happening?' And then Sasha: 'Why did you call me?' Sasha was actually in my room with me, in person, but he was his comics character; I saw his drawing of himself, but I was not surprised by this sight, it was all perfectly normal to me. Then the rest of the dialogue: G: 'I did not call you, you were here.' S: 'I was dreaming, and you called me here.' G: 'Maybe I'm dreaming, too. Look, I don't wear pajamas when I sleep, and now I have some, and they're so ugly!' S: 'Perhaps I called you here. Look, I am a cartoon.' G: 'No, Sasha, you look pretty fine, as usual.' S: 'Yes, but I must come back home now.' G: 'And how shall we do that? You are the dream-travels expert.' S: 'Don't know. Try to erase me, or take off those pajamas.' G: 'Mmmmh, I'll try the first one.' And then I made a gesture with my hand, as if I were de-misting a glass. I woke up. Pretty mystic, isn't it?"

Funniest thing of all, I haven't had many interesting dreams since the war started. I feel pretty vacant, and all that I can see in my dreams is a big black void. I know it's too negative, but I wonder if this phantasmagoric war reality is disturbing my ability to concentrate on dream experiences
Good night Sasa

64 people and just one house
Mon, 24 May 1999 17:23:06

Hello! The reason why I haven't written before, or why your messages sent to me probably bounced, is because the power plants in Serbia were exposed to NATO bombings – they were using both "soft" and old fashioned "heavy" bombs, and we spent past few days mostly in the dark, and during the times when the power came up again, it wasn't possible to connect to the internet.

I should say that I made a mistake in my last letter, as it turned out that the bomb that fell in the fields near Banatski Brestovac was not dropped on the anti-aircraft defenses, as I had guessed. I saw a report about the local tractor drivers who watched, appalled, as an aircraft dropped a bomb on a soybean plant, a couple of hundred metres away. It seems that it was one of the bombs which, for some reason, were not used against the planned target, and the NATO planes – unable to land with bombs still attached to them – have to kick them out somewhere. A lot of the bombs were, therefore, dropped in the Adriatic sea near Italy, Croatia and (probably) Monte Negro, and in the fields of Macedonia, etc. Once they start throwing bombs, there is just no end to incidents like this, bombs are everywhere.

The other day we visited some friends in a village near Pancevo – they told us that during the crisis caused by NATO bombings of the industrial zone of the town, almost all of the houses in a village were full of city people who were trying to escape to the countryside. They spoke about their friends who gave shelter to the members of their numerous family, so that at one point there were 64 people in their humble home!!! It was too crowded to sleep on the beds and chairs and on the floor, so mostly they would just sit and talk throughout the night, and sleep for a few hours during the day. When they became tired of it all, they decided that the grown-ups should leave and find shelter with some other relatives, so that there would be more space left for the children. So the house ended up with "only" 30 kids dwelling it!!!

They said that at least 1 million people in Serbia were forced to leave their homes, permanently or for a time being. For a population of 10 million people, that is quite a lot. OK, I got to try to send this while we still have the power.
Until soon Sasa

Hello! For the past few days, troubles with black outs are the things that most of people here have been talking about. After the use of special, brand new bombs with carbon filaments, NATO has day after day been destroying the basic infrastructure (with "old fashioned" bombs) used in the production and distribution of power in Serbia – power plants, transformer stations, etc. As many of you probably never experienced major black outs, maybe it's good to describe what it looks like, actually. First of all, most of people do not have water during the black outs, as the pumps can not distribute it. And even when aggregates are being used, people living in the upper floors of the apartment buildings (like Gordana and I do) are left without water.

Also, frozen food supplies are being spoiled, and have to be thrown on the dump, in the midst of the crisis. Many people in Belgrade are donating the food which is not edible any more (for humans, at least) to the local zoo. Not to mention the problem of hospitals, bakeries, factories, or families with new born babies, being cut off from power. Can you imagine what is it is like when somebody who's living in a tall building DIES during the black outs? (Yes, it happens).

Spending many hours in dark, every night, while aircraft are bombing your town, is a kind of creepy experience. They don't even have to switch out Serbia from the internet, as the internet connections in this situation are becoming more and more disrupted. (By the way, if you emailed me and the message bounced, please be patient, and send it again!!!)

The funny thing is that if you leave almost an entire country in the dark, it simply does not sound as awful as killing people with bombs, so destruction of a power network will never cause such a big sensation in the Western media, even though it is a measure which hurts millions of people.

"The covers of all the magazines here have pictures of the 'Star Wars' movie – no mentions of Yugoslavia", wrote Chris Ware, in his most recent

letter: "I wish I could say 'the world's gone nuts' but I think that it's always been this way; it's just an endless variation on a theme and we're simply artists who are silly enough to think that things should be different."
See you Sasa

No compromises?
Sat, 29 May 1999 00:11:23

Hello to all!

May 27th 1999. After the snail mail from abroad stopped being delivered to Serbia, I almost stopped visiting a post office to check out my P.O. box. And when I finally went there to check it out, it turned out that a book, ordered before this madness began, somehow managed to get through!!! I ordered it from Bud Plant's catalogue, and it is a handsome "MAD about the Fifties" volume, with all the classic strips from the early *Mad* magazine. Hooray! A new book on my table. Can't believe it! All those genuine concepts by H. Kurtzman! Glorious stuff by Elder, Wolverton, Wood, Davis and all the others!!!! American satire from the 50s was so sharp, so beautifully executed. We should all learn from it, for many years to come. It is a great literature to read under the light of the candle during the black-outs.

May 28th 1999. Yesterday, the power went off shortly after the booming sound of a bomber plane was heard over our neighborhood. NATO has destroyed some of the important power plants near Belgrade. The power comes off and on again, every now and then.

A few hours ago, NATO bombed a garbage dump near Pristina, with four projectiles. Whatever the real target was, you can add a garbage dump to the list of the bombed places and objects in Serbia. Of course, everybody here is talking about Milosevic being indicted for war crimes. Just at the moment when some agreement for the halt of the military action in Kosovo was about to be settled through diplomacy, lead by Russians! It seems that NATO, which has a very strong influence on the policy of the War Crimes Tribunal in Hague, simply does not want to appear ready to make any compromises, and is more eager to continue with the pressure against the "enemy". Is it even more important than to stop the suffering of both Albanian and Serbian civil population? I've been discussing these things with Donna Barr, who is able to very sharply analyze and understand the military logic, as you can see from her well-researched comics set inside the WW2 milieu.

"There is a lot of media talk about Milosevic 'cracking'", said Donna: "This is American media-talk for 'He is willing to negotiate'. In American culture, there are only complete winners or complete losers; one is not allowed to compromise. It is a sign of 'weakness'. Many of our people suffer from stress-illness because they cannot 'win completely' all the time. And do you know what the British said? That Milosovic has 'back up generators', and if 'he' is choosing to use 'his' generators for the military instead of the hospitals, then it's 'his' headache. You are no longer a country to NATO – you are one person. YOU are all to be treated as that one person. And repeatedly we see oil refineries burning. This is an OIL question again."

Speaking of compromises, it is something quite unpopular within a military logic in just any country. There is a joke, that I heard here in Serbia, about Milosevic writing a letter to Clinton: "Dear Bill, we can't take it any more. It's about time for you to surrender"!!!!
That's all for now, Sasa

Poison ivy
Sat, 29 May 1999 22:13:37

Hello! The other day we met Zoran Jovic-Djavo, a drummer in a band called NUP, and an author of several mini comics (working under the pseudonym of Letac). He was drafted, and is stationed with the anti-aircraft defenses in the farms near his native village. He gave me a funny souvenir – a piece of one of the bombs that fell near the village. Djavo said that one of the officers noticed that he was searching through the remains of the bomb. "What are you looking for?" – asked the officer. "I would like to have a little souvenir", said Djavo. "The most interesting part is the wing. If you want, take it. But be careful, they said that some

The 'caged' exhibition of *Life Under Sanctions*

of the bombs are radioactive". The officer even helped to dismantle the "wings". But soon Djavo's wrist became red, and he started to scratch. Was it because of the radioactivity!? He rushed to the officer in panic, and showed him his wrist all red, and the officer started to shout: "Don't come any closer!!! You are CONTAMINATED"!!! But just a minute later, he started to laugh, and explained that it was a trick: the officer has scratched Djavo's wrist with the poison ivy! Military humor.

While speaking to Djavo about his experiences, one of the most eerie moments that he remembered was when NATO aircraft on one occasion has lit up everything underneath, in order to spot the target. The night landscape was lit so suddenly and from such a powerful source of light, and it was almost as shocking as the bombing itself. Another friend, Damir Smit, who is running a comics workshop in Subotica, is the only male person that we know who succeeded to get out of the country during the war. After a lot of efforts, he was given permission from the Army Headquarters to go to Slovenia and take part in the Art Festival, called Break 21. While on his way home, Damir stayed in Hungary for a few days. "Budapest is full of people who are speaking Serbian" – he said. "It is only the latest of many waves of war immigrants from Serbia, mostly young people trying to avoid draft".

I was also informed that Triceps, one of the most famous alternative artists in Budapest, has set up an exhibition in his underground gallery, with enlarged pages of my "Life Under Sanctions" strip, placed behind ancient bars in the basement. I saw the photos, it looks very interesting. I wish that I was able to go to Budapest and chat with Triceps. We are all the prisoners of the situation here.

See you soon Sasa

BOMB THE BRIDGES!
Mon, 31 May 1999 17:35:00

Hello! Well, well, we can see that the NATO bombing campaign is intensifying again.

Yesterday morning, we heard a strong detonation. It seemed that the whole apartment building was shaking, and everybody guessed that it was a projectile that had fallen in the Pancevo area. The area which was rocketed was in fact some 20 to 30 km away, which means that very powerful projectiles were used. I can only imagine what it felt like in the targeted area. There were countless NATO attacks during the night and day yesterday, but the most awful, most frightening one was in a quiet little town of Varvarin, where the small bridge in the centre was bombed while civilian traffic was flowing across it. It was a market day, and an

Orthodox Christian holiday, and the town was full of people who came from the surrounding area. The strike was renewed just a few minutes later, while passers-by were coming to the rescue of the people who were injured by the first strike! (I guess that the pilot must have seen that the bridge was crowded with civilians and their vehicles?) Eleven people were found dead, and 40 injured, but as the traffic was very busy, and many vehicles fell in the river, the real number of victims of this glorious action will yet to be defined. As we learned from the similar cases when the bridges were bombed by NATO in this war; some of the bodies were found floating in the river several weeks after the bombing. And still, NATO officials have already confirmed that the bridge was a "legitimate military target". OK, OK, just do your job, guys, we still believe that it is a humanitarian mission you're on.

This morning, around 4AM, we were awakened by the hissing sound of Cruise missiles. I woke up to listen to the detonations coming from the direction of Belgrade.

As the power plants were hit again last night, the possibility of retaining proper delivery of electrical power in Serbia is shrinking. Everybody is thinking about the upcoming winter, and even Gordana and I are trying to figure out what to do, as – probably – there will be no fuel for heating. Also, food supplies will start to vanish soon. In order to use meat stored in freezers, affected during black-outs, a lot of families are holding barbecues while it is still edible. Speaking of meat, Gordana is cooking, so I had better go eat.
Goodbye for now, Sasa

First day of June
Tue, 1 Jun 1999 22:13:41

Hello everybody! It's June already, and we are still living under the bombs. Last night, as usual, NATO has bombed the power plants, and then around midnight, while everything for miles around was covered by darkness, Pancevo was bombed again. It was the empty Army barracks in the Northern part of the town again, as many as 8 projectiles were fired in a series of strikes. It was so meaningless. When they bomb during the black outs, everything is silent, and the sound of the explosions radiates through the open spaces. To me, it sounded like each blast echoed with something empty, pointless inside. There was another NATO strike in the area last night, targeting the anti-aircraft defenses in the near-by village of Omoljica. Anti-aircraft weaponry has to be constantly moved, in order to avoid NATO counter-attacks. The attack happened while anti-aircraft defenses were close to some local farm, and, according to gossips, some soldiers were killed, and some were injured as well.

The whole atmosphere in this land is pretty depressive – many people are losing their jobs, and most of those who are working get their salaries after a great delay (if they get any salary at all), and most of the people are spending their life savings, and it's hard to tell how much longer they will be able to carry on like that. Gordana told me that some people were fired from the company where she works and an awful thing happened just a few days ago, when one of those who was left without a job, 32 years old, woke up one night, took a gun, and killed his grandmother, mother, and father – while they were sleeping, and then committed suicide. So many families in Serbia must be in a critical condition right now, even though most of them seem to be trying to cope with the situation, to survive, to carry on somehow.

See you Sasa

Happy Gypsies
Wed, 2 Jun 1999 22:39:12

Hello! Last night there was an explosion, which made some strange noise, reminding me of the crack of a giant whip. It turned out that the bomb fell very close to our part of the town, less then 500 metres from our home, close to the road which leads from Pancevo to Belgrade. The bomb probably missed its target (the industrial zone is not so far away), or its direction was changed by a hit from anti-aircraft defenses. Anyway, the bomb fell close to the "favela" type Gypsy settlement, called Mali Rit, but also known as "Mali London" (Little London). It is a place where one of

the best Serbian movies (to my taste) was filmed, in 1967 – "Happy Gypsies" was its name (originally: "Skupljaci perja", which means Feather Collectors"), directed by late Aleksandar Petrovic. It was a while before the movies about Gypsies became "fashionable". The settlement was much larger in the 60s, but in the early 70s the City Government probably concluded that it was bad propaganda for a town, and most of the people who lived there were moved to a "solid" houses, and their original settlement was destroyed. Still, in the past few decades, many of the Romany people came back to the legendary "Little London", and built their humble homes there. Just a few years ago, Gordana and I were helping the Italian NGO "Razzismo Stop" to deliver humanitarian aid there. After the explosion, one woman was injured by broken glass, and Pancevo's Mayor came to visit the place – I saw him on the local TV report,and while he was showing off the shrapnel found on site, you could hear the laughter of "Little London's" inhabitants. They were still joking and posing in front of the camera, and one woman said: "Bombing hasn't done any harm to our house. We were lucky that we just have a nylon sheets instead of glass windows!" I also recognized my school mate Sava Novakov, who was quite close to the place where the bomb fell. Sava had a career in boxing, he even won some medals in international competitions. In recent years, he dropped boxing completely, and it was good to see him still joking, even in this occasion.

I was thinking about that old song from the band called Azra: "We, the Gypsies, are damned by one fate: Every now and then Somebody comes and threatens us."

See you tomorrow Sasa

When the leaflets fly
Thu, 3 Jun 1999

Hello! Today we went to pick black cherries at my parents' garden. While we were busy, Gordana saw a NATO leaflet on the ground. Soon, there were more leaflets falling from the sky – they were obviously thrown from an aircraft, which is funny, because there were no air raid sirens, which are supposed to warn about the presence of NATO planes. I found 4 new different types of leaflets, which was fun.

One of the pamphlets contains a quote from the open letter to Milosevic published a few months ago, and co-written by Slavko Curuvija, a journalist killed shortly after the NATO bombing campaign started: "You have destroyed the spirit of tolerance by inventing conflicts, and by pushing confrontation between rich and the poor, towns and villages, between Serbia and Monte Negro, police and the army. You turned the professors against the students, illiterate against literate people"

The leaflet ends with the conclusion: TODAY, THE SITUATION IS EVEN WORSE. Later we saw the children running through the fields, and all over town, and collecting the leaflets.

A friend told me that he saw the leaflets falling on the central market in Pancevo, while the place was crowded with people. So many passers-by were running to catch the pamphlets, and somebody said:" It looks as if they are throwing dollar bills", because of the format of the leaflets. Anyway, it's good that not only bombs are falling from the NATO planes. Leaflets are more fun.

Regards Sasa

EUROPE 93
Sat, 5 Jun 1999 zograf@panet.bits.net

Hello people! Well, every day brings a hope that this silly war is going to end somehow. Milosevic has accepted the peace plan, and today it was reported that Serbian Army officials and NATO generals have met in a little bar called "Evropa 93" (Europe 93) at the Serbo-Macedonian border. It was funny to see such an "important" event going on at a local bar, with about 300 journalists from all the major press agencies waiting in front of it. Still, still – NATO continues to bomb towns all over Serbia. Yesterday, 15 towns were targeted. This morning, they bombed the fields in the outskirts of the neighboring town of Vrsac, and one tractor-driver was seriously injured when blast kicked him out of the vehicle's cabin. Vrsac is a town where Wostok – the infamous Serbian cartoonist, and a good friend of mine lives. I just received couple of his new comic fanzines, including another of the crazy "porno" (or is it a parody of pornography?) stories that Wostok has done in collaboration with his 70-something year old father!!! By the way, Wostok's wife works as a nurse in a mental hospital in Vrsac. Her job is very delicate, as she works (with another colleague) at the female section of the special ward, where the patients who are aggressive or whose behavior could be dangerous to the other patients are hospitalized. Even during the air raids, she is supposed to stay locked in the ward, and she can only let the patients leave in case of extreme emergency. Luckily, Vrsac was bombed on just a few occasions, but after one of the detonations, the glass in the windows of the Mental Hospital were broken, and one patient, a woman (not in a ward where Wostok's wife Natasa works) was overwhelmed by panic and jumped out of the window (from the first floor). The poor woman broke her leg, but Natasa said that, generally speaking, most of the patients have been accepting the war situation pretty well (even though there is a shortage of medication left over from the times of economic sanctions against Serbia in 1993). By the way, yesterday we spoke to a neighbor who was drafted and serves as a mechanic with a local army unit in Pancevo. He said that the anti-aircraft artillery which they are using to match the mighty 21st Century NATO airplanes was made in 1962!!? This all sounds like a parody, but – YES – that is the reality in this somnambulist country.

Bye Sasa

Coo Coo!
Mon, 7 Jun 1999

Hello! Yes, this is all insane – the deal between NATO and Serbian generals has fallen through this morning, after Serbian generals rejected the NATO plan, proposed to them in ultimatum-like manner. During the days and hours while the peace is postponed, many soldiers and civilians will die, and the rest will sit helplessly in tents far away from home. Today, we were receiving contradictory information: yes, the plan is going to be accepted sometime soon! No, it is not! This official from the Serbian side said that. That NATO general said something else. And so on. In the meantime, NATO declared this morning that they will continue to intensify their bombing campaign, and this afternoon several people were killed, and many more were injured today, after what seemed to be a pause in the bombing. The whole stupid war may go on forever, and even if it stops tomorrow, it will not be the end of trouble for the people living in this country. Just as I was writing this message, around midnight, NATO struck Pancevo again, and several very heavy bombs fell on the oil refinery. The sound of the explosion was mixed with the sound of breaking glass. We spoke to a woman from the flat below us, and she said that their lamp in the hall was broken to pieces. The smashing sounds were heard all over neighborhood. There were several more strikes, and loud explosions, and we were able to see projectiles falling on suburban parts of Belgrade as well – at least two projectiles, eerily, slowly hovering above the ground, were hit by anti-aircraft defenses. It was like a battle in the sky. Strangely, the strikes were followed by a sudden stormy wind, which seemed to be awoken by all the hassle in the sky.

Gordana and I went at the top of our apartment building, where there was our neighbor who is a TV cameraman, and beside his camera he was equipped with a pocket radio station, so we were able to listen to information about the direction of the moving of the NATO aircraft, about the missiles destroyed by anti-aircraft defenses, about targets hit by NATO, just as it was happening, all over Serbia. From time to time, these reports were interrupted by a high-pitched voice of a guy from neighboring Croatia, who would toss in the comments like: "You are so stupid. You must be Serbs, aren't you?" and "Coo-Coo! NATO is coming to Tomahawk you!". Everybody calls that guy "Coo Coo", and he breaks in the Serbian amateur radio broadcasts every night, with his sarcastic comments. He became a sort of "mascot" of this war. All the while, the oil refinery was burning, there were four or five separate flames bursting out, and the giant cloud raised again over the town. Pieces of soot were falling all over the place, and we were wondering what happened to our hopes for peace. Regards Sasa

Bomb in the backyard
Wed, 9 Jun 1999 zograf@panet.bits.net

Hello to all! After last night's bombing of the oil refinery in Pancevo, our part of town is full of small soot-like sheets that lie on the ground – I heard that it could be remains of the paint from the oil tanks that were bombed. When you pick up these little black sheets from the ground, they usually just fall apart. Last night, at the top of our building, somebody saw something that looked like a big block of shiny black material, hovering above the 8 storey building. It seems that materials from the oil refinery were launched for kilometres around! One of the cameramen, who was present at the site just 15 minutes after the strike, told our friend that the giant flame in the oil refinery has been sucking up a big quantity of oxygen, so that he felt that he was attracted by the fire in a most unusual way, and that any minute he could be sucked inside it. He compared that experience to "being swallowed by a whirlwind".

This morning when I went outside it seemed to me at first that it was cloudy weather that was hiding the sun on the horizon. It took me a few moments to realize that what was spreading in the sky above was in fact an enormous black cloud, coming out of the oil refinery. Last time during a similar NATO action against the same plant in Pancevo, the big cloud traveled 1000's of kilometres away from Serbia, reaching as far as Scandinavia! One of the "specialties" of the previous oil refinery bombing was a "black rain" that fell on Pancevo, and it is possible that the same thing will happen today as well.

I heard on the news that two of the NATO projectiles that fell on Belgrade last night haven't actually exploded. One of the projectiles that fell in a part of town called Kotez has crashed through the roof of a private house, and landed in the backyard unexploded.

A similar incident occurred ten days ago, when a NATO projectile hit a house not so far away from the centre of Belgrade, while a mother and her son were inside, and they were not hurt by some miracle, even though the living room was completely destroyed. The bomb, unexploded, eventually landed in the backyard, eight metres under the ground! Specialists are still trying to dismantle it, without much success, because of the difficult position of the projectile. For 10 days, the whole neighborhood is living with the knowledge that the bomb is still with them, a few dozen metres away from their homes. Who would even think that things like that could happen.

See you soon Sasa

Peace?
Thu, 10 Jun 1999

Hello! It finally happened!!!

Yesterday, all the media in Yugoslavia were speaking of the peace agreement that was signed by Serbian and NATO generals. It was announced with a lot of triumphalism, like – "We won!". Serbian media even lied that it was UN representatives who were negotiating with Serbian Army officials, while trying to avoid mentioning NATO as the real partner in these talks. The same kind of logic (newspaper headlines like "Serbia capitulated!") was, as I understood from the letters by friends from abroad, present in the mainstream media of NATO countries. They were opening champagne at the NATO headquarters in Brussels. After so many (whatever the real number is) thousands of dead and injured and people left homeless?

Yes, yes, it was so predictable. I told you that it would happen, in one of my early messages – politicians will continue to do their "job", they will make speeches, pose in front of the camera, or at worst transfer to a new duty – no matter what the result of their fabulous "action". They are the "winners" – Serbian, Albanian, NATO leaders, and the busy little administration workers. These guys always win. Everybody else is wounded or dead.

Anyway, this is the last of my mass letters, unless something goes wrong again.

Yesterday, the "celebration" started with people from the neighborhood taking their pistols and shooting in the air. They were joined by rockets launched by anti-aircraft defenses, even though at first I thought that they were shooting at the pilotless NATO aircraft (equipped with cameras), as they usually do when they are shooting between air raids. I just couldn't believe that they would waste the rockets that they actually didn't use while combating the mighty NATO bombers. Sure, everybody was happy that the whole thing was over. Even though many were complaining, and many more were aware that this is far from being the end of the crisis – ANYTHING could happen in the months to come. The "victory" celebration in my town was ridiculed by the tall flame from the oil refinery, and the giant black cloud which was spreading over the whole area. The industrial complex is still burning, even now as I write this, 3 days after the NATO bombing.

But still, I can understand the triumph of the common people, who were exposed to the very powerful bombs for 77 days. They are the real heroes! The same is true with the common Albanians, who suffered enormously in this big turmoil. Serbia will be a country which will enter the 21st Century with destroyed factories, bridges, railroads and highways. No matter the high ideals of our world, global society is still obsessed with deeply destructive and violent concepts. Isn't it obvious yet?

See you around, my friends.

Sasa

AFTERWORD

June 26th 1999.

After the NATO bombing campaign against targets in Serbia was over, and international troops (KFOR) entered Kosovo, it was supposed to be the "end" of something. The end of the war, or something like that. But it is really hard to see the beginning or the end in this situation. And again it was so predictable. Now, as the result of revenge attacks by ethnic Albanians, the remaining Serbs from Kosovo are being robbed and killed and kicked out of their homes, and the KFOR troops are mostly just standing by, with all their expensive equipment and modern weaponry, and watching as the Serbian houses are set on fire, and tens of thousands of Serbian refugees are leaving their homes. It was hard to expect KFOR to react harshly toward Kosovo Liberation Army atrocities, as just a few weeks ago they were the allies – with members of the KLA using satellite phones to send information about Serbian Army targets to NATO. Still, it is most probable that sooner or later, to one degree or another, KFOR (as some sort of substitute for the police) will have to clash with the KLA, who were largely sponsored by organized crime, and who were regularly killing Serbian civilians and policemen, and disobedient ethnic Albanians as well, long BEFORE the NATO bombing campaign even started. Another problem is that a lot of people from Northern Albania, who never even lived in Kosovo, are now coming there and jumping into other people's houses. It is sad to see all the press men who came to find mass graves, and the saddest thing is that they really ARE going to find them after all. Whoever the dead people are, Albanians or Serbs or others; the national leaders are celebrating: Milosevic is giving boastful speeches, proclaiming victory and the beginning of the renewal of our destroyed country; the ethnic Albanian leadership is parading with weapons and flags – celebrating their own victory; and NATO officials are proudly giving triumphant press conferences in the heart of towns which were bombed, burnt, robbed or deserted. It makes you want to throw up. Anyway, the chaos in Kosovo is a painful example of how the terms of "good and bad" can be mixed and deformed in conflicts like this.

My wife Gordana just came in with news about her neighbor, who lived next door to her old place ever since she was born, and who was drafted to serve as a mechanic with the Army units around Pancevo. As the Serbian Army started to withdraw from the territory of Kosovo, he was sent there to fix some of the vehicles. He joined the Army column on his way back home, but the KLA had set a trap for them, and shot with snipers, despite the official cease fire. Gordana's friend was brave enough to jump from the truck while his friend who was at the wheel was shot dead. The result of this "action" was two soldiers killed, and two seriously injured, including Gordana's friend – after he jumped out of the truck he was shot and the bullet literally passed through his chest, taking out a piece of his lungs. He is now recovering in a hospital in Belgrade, and his friends and relatives still don't want to tell his mother about the incident. In fact, incidents like this are kept secret, and you can't find reports about it anywhere in the Serbian media. As for lighter subjects, I'm still trying to turn my attention back to comics. But it's not always easy, simply because you have to adjust to life in a country where nothing is the same as it used to be.

Sasa Rakezic
Pancevo, Serbia

ICE CREAM IN THE DUMP

Still, for many hours during the day, we are left without the power and running water. As you can guess, it is really bad for the food supplies we stored in refrigerators and freezers.

I like to eat sweet (like a baby!), and it breaks my heart to hear about the cake shop supplies of ice cream that had to be thrown away in the dump, in the midst of the crisis...

As I said before, the Belgrade's zoo is placed within the remains of the city's old fortification, pretty close to the main pedestrian street, called Knez Mihajlova. The people who run the zoo were trying to solve the problem of large and dangerous animals running away from the zoo, in case of the fortification being bombed.

So during the air raids, there is a gun squad coming to the zoo, ready to shoot the animals... First they were thinking about putting the animals to sleep, but the serum just lasts for several hours, and nobody knows what might happen in the case of bombing.

(As it was the case in the World War 2, when wild animals were running all over the streets of Belgrade, together with the people bewildered by "carpet bombing".)

Speaking of bombings, they are still finding out the bodies under the ruins of the houses in a small town of Surdulica, a week after the NATO had bombed the civilian block of houses...

It was a horrible event, with most of the victims being children, hiding in a shelter. The bodies were torn to pieces, and it was very hard to identify them.

It was reported that two more people committed suicide, after this event...

According to the information that I heard on Radio Free Europe, the number of the Serbs fleeing from Kosovo is, proportionally, even bigger than the number of Albanians.

Everybody seems to running away from the place, except for the men in uniforms, and that is so frightening...

OK, I'm trying to send this before another black-out...

Regards

Sasa

Emailed by Sasa Rakezic, Pancevo, 6 MAY 1999.   drawn by David Lasky MAY/JUNE

Comic strip created by David Lasky from one of Sasa's emails

ALL AROUND THE WORLD

The emails were posted onto a number of sites, in many languages. They also appeared in the Italian print media (periodicals such as *Il Manifesto, La Stampa, Cuore, Rumore*) – Italian public opinion was greatly opposed to the war. The websites included:

Danish: www.hib.dk/~dadk/

English: www.eosdev.com/serbia.htm

www.comicon.com/ubb/Forum1/HTML/000333.html

www.parascope.com/articles/cnews/index

Italian: www.fumetti.org/novita.htm

www.peacelink.it/Kossovo/lettere/sasa

http://moebius.freeweb.org

http://giramondo.com/osservatorio/guerra/diario

www.partitoumanista.org/eventi/lettereserbia/

www.fucine.com

Japanese: www.geocities.co.jp/Hollywood/

In addition artist Maaike Hartjes has compiled an excellent site of diary style strips, adapting the emails of Sasa and another Serbian cartoonist and her own reponses and reactions into comic form (Dutch text). This work can be found at:

www.melenhorst.demon.nl/oorlogstrip/

French and Italian versions of this book have been published. They are:

E-Mails de Pancevo, ISBN 2-84414-018-1, 49FF from L'Association, 16 rue de la Pierre Levee, 75011, Paris, France

Lettere dalla Serbia, ISBN 88-86945-19-1, 14500L from Editrice PuntoZero, Via San Pier Tonasso 18/d, 40139 Bologna, Italy

The "Regards From Serbia" strips appeared in papers such as *New City, The Austin American-Statesman, The Stranger, Vancouver Sun*, on the ComicStore.com web site, and in European magazines - *Linus* (Italy) and *Babel* (Greece).

ALSO BY ALEKSANDAR ZOGRAF

Dream Watcher
ISBN 1 899866 13 2
The definitive collection of Zograf's work, covering both his "war report" strips and his explorations of dreams and hypnagogic visions.
£5.00/$9.95 from Slab-O-Concrete, PO Box 148, Hove, BN3 3DQ, UK

Psychonaut #3
The latest Zograf comic, all new work that reveals the thin boundary between reality and the dream world in depressed ex-Yugoslavia.
$3.50 from Monsterpants Comics, PO Box 1122, Burbank, CA, 91507 USA or £2.50 from Slab-O-Concrete for UK customers.

Psychonaut #1 & #2 and
Life Under Sanctions
$4.00 post paid from Fantagraphics Books, 7563 Lake City Way NE, Seattle, WA 98115, USA

Psychonaut
German editions. 9,95DM from Jochen Enterprises, Mockernstr. 78, 10965, Berlin, Germany

Psychonaut T-Shirts
£7.00 from Slab-O-Concrete

Diaro
4000 Lira from Schizzo, Via Speciano 2, 26100 Cremona, Italy

Alas! Comics #1–6 and
Hypnagogic Review #1–2
Self-published by Zograf himself. $2 from Sasa Rakezic, PF 163, 26000 Pancevo, Yugoslavia. *Alas!* #1 available in Italian (ask for Edizione Italiana). Please send cash only.